THE FIELDS OF
Gomorrah

STACEY HERRING

Fields of Gommorah
Copyright ©2023 Stacey Herring

Published by Castle Quay Books
Burlington, Ontario, Canada and Jupiter, Florida, U.S.A.
416-573-3249 | info@castlequaybooks.com | www.castlequaybooks.com

Printed in Canada

Edited by Marina Hofman, PhD

All rights reserved. This book or parts thereof may not be reproduced in any form without prior written permission of the publishers.

This is a work of fiction. Names, characters, businesses, places, events and incidents are either the products of the author's imagination or used in a fictitious manner. Any resemblance to actual persons, living or dead, or actual events is purely coincidental.

Unless otherwise indicated, all Scripture quotations are taken from the King James Version of the Bible. • Scripture quotation marked (NIV) is taken from the Holy Bible, New International Version®, NIV® Copyright ©1973, 1978, 1984, 2011 by Biblica, Inc.® Used by permission. All rights reserved worldwide.

978-1-998815-02-9 Soft Cover
978-1-998815-03-6 E-book

CIP catalog record information for the Library of Congress is available from the publisher.

Library and Archives Canada Cataloguing in Publication
Title: The fields of Gomorrah : a gripping story exposing the dark world of human trafficking /
  written by Stacey Herring.
Names: Herring, Stacey, author.
Identifiers: Canadiana (print) 20230550908 | Canadiana (ebook) 20230550916 | ISBN 9781998815029
  (softcover) | ISBN 9781998815036 (EPUB)
Subjects: LCGFT: Novels.
Classification: LCC PS3608.E78 F54 2023 | DDC 813/.6—dc23

CASTLE QUAY BOOKS

Stacey Herring

It's funny to me how we move along with time. Like fish in the stream, we just ... flow. We live our everyday life and do our everyday things. And time goes on. And then, on occasion, we pop out of the water and ask, "What else is there?"

Life gives. Life takes. Broken dreams. Loss of health and people we love. In my marriage of twenty-six years, my husband and I have walked some difficult roads.

What I have learned from him is to never give up on what God is telling you to do. No matter how much you would like to.

I began writing this story in 2019. My family had just finished our first battle with my breast cancer, and I decided it was time to truly pursue that which was knit in me from my youth.

With both my wonderful daughters' support and my amazing husband Brian's inspiration and encouragement driving me forward, I persisted in completing my first novel. He seemed to speak the exact words of encouragement I needed when my self-talk was dripping with defeat.

And then there was the eleven-year-old girl inside of me, cheering me on, reminding me of what I really wanted to do with my life regarding a career. My marriage is a dream come true. My children, Molly and Ellie, are my pride and joy. And while I had been in ministry for more than ten years, there was something in me—something that felt undone. A story to be told. A talent to be used.

It was exciting to think that I was still capable of following a God-sized calling. I was in a unique time of life. Cancer was behind me, and I was slowly feeling the effects of treatment subside. Life was returning to busy. I had all the important responsibilities in front of me. People that depended on me that I wanted to give my time to. I wanted to pursue the dream—but the timing wasn't yet.

Then cancer returned.

I was so close to the five-year window. Stage 4 this time. Metastasized. In the bone. No cure. No way to fight. So said the medical industry. But I do serve a God who can do great things. And even today I trust Him for a great story!

There is a powerful concept that I hope is clearly conveyed in this book. It is important to realize that though we may not consider ourselves capable of greatness—never the ones rescuing children, receiving the highest honors, or creating important cures—we are all so very capable. A willing heart and a life in line with God's will—that is a powerful partnership! When everyday people seek to align themselves with the awe-inspiring Creator God—magnificent, unbelievable things begin to happen!

I love that I am a modest girl, from a small town in Ohio. I love that I am the seventh child (not the baby!). I love that God has purpose for my gifts every day and that one of those is a gift with words. I love that my story is not finished until the Author and Finisher declares it so with my dying breath.

I have learned through the loss of parents, the loss of health, and a real struggle with my faith that God is sovereign in all things. He has shown me that He can complete what He began, if I allow Him. His grace pours over me constantly, and I know I need it. I need to stay there, in that place—close to Him. Focusing on Him. Choosing Him.

And while I may be in the time of life when many may consider themselves washed up—I am reminded that God Himself is writing my story. It's not over; there is still so much to do. And it is *good!*

With so many friends and family rooting me on, thanking everyone will prove to be quite the task. But here goes: Thank you ...

Brian, the best husband a girl could ever dream of having—you encourage me by example and your tireless effort of relentlessly pursuing what God has put in you.

Molly and Ellie, my girls—I pray you are encouraged by the good things I do and find in yourselves the ability to do God inspired things.

April, my longest supporter—your faith in me since high school has been unwavering.

Dawn D.—your prayers and encouragement have covered me.

Cheri—no better cheerleader to push me forward than you, my friend.

My siblings—for the way we continuously support and believe in one another, despite our differences. Or maybe because of them.

Dawn B.—for conspiracies, conversation, and connections!

My newest friends, Larry and Marina—for your faith in me and for your willingness to shine light on a devastating issue in our society. Thank you for bringing this story to print.

Carrie P.—Are you ready for our next assignment?!

Though I walk through the valley of the shadow of death,
I will fear no evil;
For You are with me.
(Psalm 23:4, NKJV)

Beth Everett tossed back and forth. She had seen this girl in her dreams before.

It was dark. From what Beth could make out, the girl looked to be fifteen or sixteen. Behind her was a barren field filled with dead stalks and fallow ground. Her face was bloodied and bruised, her blond hair waving in a soft breeze.

Her slight frame moved among the shadows. She was reaching, reaching.

"Is she reaching for me?" Beth couldn't get to the girl. She was too far away.

Beth thought she heard the girl's voice, but the speech was blurred, echoed. She couldn't make out the words. She tried so hard to hear.

A sense of hopelessness overwhelmed Beth. She could not reach across the chasm between dream and reality.

With one arm, the girl beckoned, reaching for Beth. In the other, the girl held a baby. Time was the enemy, and she was desperate to be heard.

Beth made out a word—

"Children!"

One

"*A three-day suspension*, Cassie, really? First, your grades slip, and you have to go to summer school. Now this?" Alexis Woods briefly stared at her daughter as she placed the white Camry in gear and backed out of the parking space.

Cassie took a deep breath as the familiar surge of anger dared to surface. She had yet to tell her side of the story. The teacher wouldn't listen, the principal wouldn't listen, and now her mom refused to hear her side of the altercation.

Her mother was typically a reasonable woman, but today's events would definitely push her to the edge.

"I just wish I could understand what you were thinking. Sarah has been your friend since third grade."

Cassie shrugged her long blond hair off her shoulder and rolled her eyes, letting the tension release with a huff. She looked out the window as they pulled away from the school. "They were jerks, Mom. Sarah changed in middle school. We haven't been close in years! Besides, someone had to do something."

"But a fight? Really? Cassie, when will you learn? You need to think things through. You cannot continue to be so impulsive!" Alexis kept her eyes on the road as they merged onto the highway. Frustration filled her tone. "A three-day suspension. I am so furious!"

"Well, maybe if you would have let me explain, then Principal Cason wouldn't have been so harsh. Gosh, Mom. Thanks for having my back." Cassie matched her mother's fury with ease. "You never listen." She mumbled the last bit, slamming against the seat and crossing her arms over her chest. She averted her gaze to the windows as parking lots and storefronts flashed by.

"Listen, you need to watch your tone with me. I'm not one of your friends. I'm your mother. Do you really think violence is what solves the world's problems?"

"No, Mom, obviously it's prayer." Cassie did nothing to hide the sarcasm.

Alexis's mouth dropped open. Cassie knew her mom well enough to assume she was screaming in her mind but chose to stop herself from saying something she would regret. Cassie also knew when it was time to stop poking. She adjusted the front seat until she was nearly lying down, leaned her head back on the headrest, and closed her eyes.

Moments passed until Mom spoke again, though tension filled each word. "Okay, Cassie, would you share your side of things please?"

Cassie returned the seat to an upright position. She studied her mother's profile, considering if her mom was actually ready to listen or if this was another "teachable moment."

"Well"—Cassie fully realized she was testing the waters—"Sarah is a real bit—"

"Language!" Alexis interrupted.

"Brat." Cassie tossed her mother another eye roll. She had really perfected them in the last three years. "Happy? She was a real *brat*. She was picking on Marina, and no one was stopping her. I mean, even the teachers wouldn't intervene."

"Cassie, sometimes we have to let the adults handle things in their own way. They are the ones in charge."

"Mom, you are not listening!" Cassie paused for a few deep breaths. She turned in her seat to face her mother. "Sarah was throwing her spaghetti at Marina. From across the room! Then she sent her friends to walk past her and whisper horrible things in her ear and walk away laughing." She was shaking her head, her hands clenched in anger. "It was just ... it was wrong, Mom. I saw Marina shrivel in her seat; tears were ready to fall ... I could not just sit by and let that happen. And when Sarah got up with her plate piled up with the remaining noodles—"

"Okay," her mother interjected. "So, things were bad for Marina, but how does that involve you? You need to know when to sit and when to stand, Cassie. You cannot fight every battle."

"Ugh," Cassie growled. *Teachable moments* ... "Mom, please. Sarah has been doing this to several girls since the year began. It's unreal. I'm sick of it, and I won't sit by anymore. Obviously. But just hear me out, okay?" She raised her hand to silence her mother's rebuke.

"Fine," Alexis conceded. "I'm listening."

"Okay." Cassie dropped her hand and continued. "So I calmly—"

Her mother raised her eyebrow.

"Yes, *calmly*, walked over to Sarah. I asked her if we could talk. After school. Behind the portables." Cassie rushed on with the story before her mother could stop her. "I was going to talk, Mom. I promise. And it started out that way."

Alexis kept her eyes on the road, glancing at her daughter as she continued to weave the tale.

"I asked Sarah what her damage was. She's turned into another person. She told me to mind my business." Cassie focused on the passing scenery but stole sideways glances to monitor her mom's reactions. "Of course, I told her I would. So long as she stopped messing with the other girls."

"And?"

Cassie evaluated her mother. Her face was calm, and she seemed fully engaged, so she kept talking.

"She told me to back off or she would teach me a lesson." Cassie scoffed. "Yeah, right. Sarah Moore teaching me a lesson." She shook her head and pressed on, scoffing. "I told her she could try."

Cassie paused to consider how to tell her mom the next bit of the story. "What I didn't see was Sarah's minions gathering around the corner. As I started to leave, they came and surrounded me."

13

Cassie smiled softly as she watched her mother fight with the smile at the corner of her mouth and her eyes softened.

Oh, good, Cassie thought. *She's beginning to understand.*

"What did you do?" her mother asked, her tone only hinting at the emotion Cassie was picking up on.

"Well, I've been a black belt for two years, Mom." Cassie was bursting with pride. "I put all that to use and beat all *five* of them." She didn't even try to hide her smile. She practically jumped in her seat as she replicated the moves she had used. "They were so embarrassed! Sarah was the only one who ratted me out. The others had *respect*." She emphasized the last word with a crack on the dashboard.

Alexis was fully smiling now. "I see." At the stoplight, Alexis turned to her daughter. "How exactly did you think that story would have helped your case with Mr. Cason?"

Cassie cocked her head. "I mean, who wouldn't be impressed with that, Mom?"

The light turned green, and Alexis hit the gas as they enjoyed the moment of laughter together. Cassie breathed a sigh of relief. *Sweet. She does understand!*

Alexis turned the car onto their street. Patches of dry dead grass dotted the lawns as the Florida sun beat down. The neighborhood kids moved their basketball game out of the street as the cars drove by. Soon they arrived at their ranch home with palm trees on either side of the driveway. Cassie sat up with her hand on the door and almost had it open as her mom placed the car in park.

"Not so fast, Cassie."

Cassie rolled her eyes again and slumped back into the seat with a huff. "Fine. What?"

"There will still be a punishment for this. I love your passion to protect, honey." Her mother reached over to touch Cassie on the shoulder.

Cassie shrugged her off and turned away. Her mother pulled her hand back, and Cassie felt a twinge of guilt for rejecting her.

Alexis continued. "But you can't fight at school and think there won't be repercussions. I'll discuss this with your dad, but don't expect to be super active for at least a week."

Cassie turned to face her mom. "But I can still go to Kendra's party, right?"

Alexis pursed her lips and raised her eyebrows. "Not likely." She talked fast. "Listen, Cassie, your actions today were your own. I know Sarah was in the wrong, but so were you. Handling things like that, not waiting for authority ... that's on you."

"Mom, it's her *sixteenth birthday*! I cannot miss my best friend's sweet sixteen. Are you kidding me right now?" Cassie's voice was a rising crescendo of pitch mixed with fury.

Alexis pulled the keys out of the car and continued speaking as she got out of the driver's seat. "I can see you are upset." She grabbed her purse and bags from the back seat. "I think it would be wise to just calm down and talk about this later. As I said, I'll talk to Dad, and we'll decide together what the appropriate punishment should be. For now, go to your room and start working—"

"It's a three-day suspension, genius." Cassie interrupted, her chin jutted forward, and her eyes narrowed in on her mother. "I can't do catch-up work."

"Watch it, Cassie," her mother stated calmly, leveling her with her eyes as she pulled her purse onto her shoulder. Cassie looked away quickly, unable to hold her mother's gaze. "Sarah isn't the only one who changed this year."

Fire filled Cassie's eyes, and her mouth dropped in disbelief. She climbed out of the car in a rage. Slamming the door with force, she charged toward the house.

Without turning back to face her mother, she yelled, "I can't believe you would compare me to Sarah. That girl is a bully and a fake. Unbelievable. I would never treat someone as mean as she does!"

She caught her mother's pointed words just before she closed the front door, "You just did."

Cassie escaped into the house, still seething and nowhere near ready to own her mistakes of the day.

Hours later, Cassie stormed into her bedroom. She fumed as she replayed in her mind the argument she'd just had with her parents. She leaned against the closed door and tapped her foot absently as the thoughts flooded her. Her best friend's sweet sixteen, and her parents were doubling down on this punishment. They had not missed each other's birthdays for twelve years.

She sat down in the armchair by the closet and almost immediately got up to pace. In her frustration, she overlooked the smiling faces from the photographs on her dresser. Reflections of love that she refused to accept in her moment of rage. They called to her as a reminder of all she had: blessings, protection, and love.

"I do everything they ask. I do something wrong one time. One. Time. I can't ever be good enough for them." Her arrogance and pride puffed her up, and she lashed out at her parents.

Making a small track around the room in her burning anger, she spoke into the air.

"She never gives me a chance! I am responsible. I always do the right thing." She felt the anger building within, tears of bitterness stinging her eyes. She settled into a dark rage. "I don't know what else I can possibly do to prove myself. She is so unreasonable! I swear I should just leave!"

Her mind screamed in warning, but her heart hardened. Her pace slowed as a thought began—a tenuous, terrible plan. "I'll run away," she whispered.

She stopped pacing, the strategy forming in her mind. A plot both terrifying and intriguing. She spoke tentatively, toying with the idea. She had money. She could just pack a bag.

No, I won't run away ... like to another state or anything, she reasoned against her fear.

"Grandpa!" she exclaimed quietly. "I'll just head to Grandpa's. Give Mom a good scare and teach her a lesson."

The bus stop wasn't far from there. She would have to go through a shady part of town, but she'd walked the path before. In the daylight. With her mom. She shrugged off the trepidation ... or was it a warning?

Either way, she sprang into action—her decision firm.

"I am out of here. Now!" Anger punched each word as she mumbled through gritted teeth. She rushed to pull her duffel bag from the closet and began to toss in some clothes. She pulled her money from the clay vase she had made in fourth-grade art class. She marched over to the window and threw it open with a force that surprised her.

She had one leg out the window when she looked back into the room. Tears began to fall as she took in the space that had been her sanctuary for fifteen years. She roughly swiped her eyes. Her stubborn will took over, and she pressed forward with her impulsive plan.

As Cassie climbed from the window, a thorny branch from the bougainvillea bush snapped back and scratched her across the cheek. She cursed and felt the blood as she smeared it across her face with the back of her hand. With the pain, her resolve hardened.

With haste and determination, she hustled down the street, imagining what her mother would do when she found her gone. Probably assume she went to Kendra's party. She pictured her mother sitting in the rocking chair praying. In her mind, Cassie scoffed, but her heart ached.

She walked at a brisk pace, at a near jog to escape the doubts that were nagging in her mind.

This is foolish. I've never been this *impulsive.*

She pulled her phone from her back pocket. *Nearly dead. I should have charged it.*

Though the streetlights burned bright against the night sky, dark oppression encompassed her. Somehow, she felt she was heading into the enemy's graveyard. Yes, it was the dark part of town that her mother always cautioned her about, but she'd be safe at her grandfather's house before midnight. Thinking of how she would convince him not to call her mother, she ran through a variety of plausible explanations. However, as the streets teemed with shady strangers, she felt her resolve begin to crumble.

Maybe I should just go back.

Deep in thought and questioning her decisions, Cassie walked past a man with near-black hair that was slicked back into a bun on top of his head. Her heart skipped a beat when his eyes landed on her. Immediately, she lowered her head but kept her focus on the world around her.

Music streamed from a party in a nearby building. Traffic raced by. People filled the streets like rats on a barge, yet he had singled her out in seconds. Like he had been watching for her.

His leather jacket and designer jeans did not fit this part of the neighborhood. The summer heat still was palpable even in the dark.

She reached for her phone again. The battery was completely dead.

The bus stop was just ahead. Her nerves were on alert when she saw the slight nod he gave. Cassie looked up through her bangs to see two large men loitering ahead. *A signal.* A large white van was parked on the side of the street. Grip tightening on her duffel bag, she picked up her pace.

But it was too late. She couldn't get the running start she needed when the strong arms wrapped around her. Her bag fell from her shoulder as they pulled her into the van. Her screams, muffled by large hands that covered her entire face, were drowned out by the city sounds. If anyone saw, no one would come to her rescue.

Now there was something over her mouth—a rag that reeked of something ... something sweet and metallic that she couldn't quite identify as she drifted away from the conscious world, falling into swirling darkness.

Two

A light smile touched Beth Everett's lips as she watched through the window as her two girls played in the backyard.

She brushed a wayward chestnut bang from her brow as she finished the last of the dishes. She softly tapped on the kitchen glass, causing the girls to look up. She blew a kiss to her daughters. At eight and ten, the sisters fought as much as they played. Today was a good day. The sun was high and bright, its warm rays filling the autumn winds. She hardly felt the pang of her recent loss. Each day brought healing. Though the dreams still came in the night.

Esther, her younger daughter, raced across the green grass that was littered with fallen leaves. Her jacket fell off her right shoulder—she insisted her clothes be loose and comfortable. A daily battle that Beth often decided against having. The same chestnut hair as her mother's was pulled into a failing ponytail. There was no hair tie that could keep up with the whirlwind that was Esther Amelia Everett. She was making up a new silly voice and telling a vibrant story as her big sister, Maggie, rolled with laughter.

Esther was a genuine comedian. *She will move mountains one day,* Beth thought. Her daughters' gifts were beginning to develop, and while Maggie was reserved, she was a strong leader. She weighed her decisions even at her young age and considered how things would play out. But Esther—she waited for no one. She would charge forward and think later … maybe. She had forced change from the day she arrived in their home.

Stacey Herring

Beth smiled. Yes, mountains would surely move out of her way. "If we both survive," she announced to the empty kitchen. A soft chuckle escaped as she turned from the window.

She dried her hands on the "A little bit of coffee and a whole lot of Jesus" dish towel hanging off the stove and stepped into the dining room. Her Bible, journal, notebook, and computer were already spread out across the farmhouse-style table. Settling into one of the side chairs, she pulled her phone from her pocket and tapped on her go-to news app. The long side of the table gave her more space to spread out as she studied yet left enough table space for the girls to eat lunch.

Scrolling through headlines, she found herself slipping into sadness. This world seemed to grow darker by the minute. Some new agenda the elites were focusing on to keep the common people from owning anything, Draven Wolfe supporting a new wave of radicals ... she needed to learn more about him. He seemed to be popping up in the news quite a bit lately.

The view out the sliding patio doors allowed her to keep a close eye on the girls, but her gaze drifted to the boxes stacked against the dining room wall. The daunting task of moving had been exhausting, and there still seemed to be so much to do. Her husband, Billy, had been patient and encouraging, but his long hours at the precinct didn't afford him the time to help with this mundane chore.

She pushed herself up and grabbed one of the boxes, telling herself she was almost finished. She listened to a podcast speaking of chilling headlines while she unpacked one of the last remaining boxes. This was a box of carefully wrapped trinkets and treasures. Little memories made of porcelain and glass. As she pulled each one out and unwrapped it with care, she set it on the table opposite her computer.

When she pulled the next item out, she faltered as she caught a glimpse of the contents. She cried out as the item dropped to the tile floor. Feeling the weight of the object in her soul, she bent to retrieve it and finished unwrapping the reminder. A plaque made from the walnut tree that had grown in the yard of their previous home. The home she could no longer stay in without thinking of that tiny infant.

"In Sweet Memory of William Patrick Everett, into the hands of our Savior. Until we meet again, my son." Tracing the engraved words with her finger, she recalled the moment her husband had given it to her. Chopping the tree down had been therapeutic for him, he had shared it with her. Creating the plaque was a kind gesture that revealed the depth of his love and understanding toward her.

She swallowed back tears. She had gone down that path too many times. To no avail. The grief counselor said it was healing to let the feelings wash over her. But she had made a successful practice of pushing them down. Busy with the girls. Busy with the house. Busy with anything that didn't bring him to mind. While it all was crumbling down around her. They needed change.

Taking a deep breath, she placed the plaque back in the box and set it aside. The remaining items would have to wait. She could only process so much at a time.

God had graciously opened the doors for them to find this new home. Every detail was a blessing. It was closer to the church. They could walk now. They had more space for the girls and a fantastic backyard. She smiled, thinking of how many wonderful memories her little family would make here.

When she returned to her laptop, the headlines made her cringe. She stood behind the chair and then bent over, scrolling through them all. A shooting in Texas, a human trafficking ring busted in Florida. Horrible people doing horrible things. She wondered how they had gotten to where they were even capable of doing such evil. Her heart broke for her children, knowing they would have to deal with the harsh cruelty of this broken world soon enough.

She thought of Pastor Carl's message this past Sunday, about the thief on the cross. She had no idea what the details of his crime were, but as she sat in the padded pew of her church, she thought about how Jesus so freely forgave him. How even in that final moment before his death, he was welcomed into heaven. She wondered if she could be so willing to forgive someone like the young man from the article she just read. The one who stormed the classroom and killed five. She just didn't see how she could. Or the men who paid for the use of children to fulfill their foul desires.

She shook off the thought and headed back to the kitchen to prepare a light snack for the girls. It all confirmed that homeschooling them was the best thing they could do.

She fell into easy conversation with her heavenly Father. Talking out loud as if to a friend seated at her kitchen table, as she pulled bread from the marble counter and began to prepare some toast for the girls with her delicious homemade strawberry jam.

"Father, I just want to make a difference. I see a hurting world, and I know You want to reach them. I don't know how, but please use me. I know there is not a lot I can do … and I know my first priority is my family. But I am here and willing, Lord. Work a miracle through me. Let me reach those around me. Help others through me, Jesus."

I will.

The words seemed to appear in her mind, at once comforting and exciting.

Heal the brokenhearted.

Beth's mind was stirred as she considered the phrase that had just popped into her head: heal the brokenhearted. Sadly, she was all too familiar with a broken heart. Setting down the jam knife, she walked back to the dining room table to search for the verse in her Bible.

Standing beside the table, she looked up the phrase and found it in Luke 4:18. Jesus was speaking, after he had returned to Nazareth. His hometown.

She read the verse out loud and then grabbed her prayer journal so she could write it down. "The Spirit of the Lord is upon me, because he hath anointed me to preach the gospel to the poor; he hath sent me to heal the brokenhearted, to preach deliverance to the captives, and recovering of sight to the blind, to set at liberty them that are bruised."

The words tugged at her mind, swirling around like leaves in the wind, tossing about looking for rest. She skimmed through her journal. From May 17, two weeks after baby Will's funeral, she found this tearstained entry:

> A bruised reed shall he not break, and the smoking flax shall he not quench: he shall bring forth judgment unto truth. (Isaiah 42:3)

> The LORD is nigh unto them that are of a broken heart; and saveth such as be of a contrite spirit. (Psalm 34:18)

Promise and pain both exploded like nuclear warheads in her mind. The memories flooded unbidden—the dreadful morning she found him lifeless in his crib. The struggle of years in conceiving him, the toll his birth took on her body—knowing she would never bear another child—only to have him taken away in his sleep. The funeral. The arguments with her mother, as both women struggled with grief. Her anger. Her pain. His promise. Fulfilled. Peace.

Heal the brokenhearted.

Beth found herself at the Savior's throne again, boldly in His presence. This time she wouldn't be brokenhearted. Somehow, she would use her experience to help heal someone who was.

———

Melody Rey pulled the whistling teapot off the stove and poured the boiling water into her white Bigfoot coffee mug. It recalled the trip she had taken with her sisters in the Pacific Northwest. Not that they had gone in search of Bigfoot, but the mug was a fun find!

She set the teapot on a trivet. The tea bag quickly turned the mug's contents a warm brown. She added honey and a little cream to the large cup and warmed her hands around it as she moseyed over to the couch, lost in thought.

She gently nudged her golden retriever, Cooper, out of her spot on the couch, setting the steaming cup onto the wooden coaster on the table beside her. She picked up her worn Bible from the coffee table and placed it on her lap. She cherished these quiet moments as she allowed the beloved pages to rustle through her fingers. She caught glimpses of highlights, underlining, and so many notes in the margins. She remembered receiving this Bible from Scott the night of their wedding. A treasure. New Bibles had come and gone over the past twenty-four years, received as gifts, given as re-gifts. This was her Bible, and all her years of walking with the Lord were documented in its pages.

With the last of her three children now a junior in high school, she found she had more free time on her hands, and that provided more time with the Lord. It was good to have this time with Him, even as she missed the busy years when they had needed her so much.

However, she did not warm up to freedom immediately. In fact, she loathed it. As the children's independence grew, she found herself alone, and she realized she hardly knew the woman she had become. She'd struggled for years to find her purpose, as the kids slowly stood on their own. What would she do? What could she do? She found she was inserting herself into their lives, offering advice that was never asked for, seeking attention, and being needy. She knew that was not who she wanted to be.

Scott encouraged her to go back to college, but she had no desire for that when turning fifty was just a few years away. But she had dabbled in glass blowing, mosaics, and a few other creative outlets. In the end, she'd settled into supporting a local food bank and soup kitchen. She found meaning in helping those who struggled to find a way out. Experience showed her that the most effective way to that path was building relationships and allowing people to share their stories. The rewards flowed in both directions then.

She ran her fingers through her hair. She smiled softly, thinking about how the Lord had answered her prayers: She sought Him for direction, and He gave her a new path. He breathed life back into her dreams and filled her with His divine purpose. Still Mom, but also Melody. His song. Now she smiled softly before bowing her head in prayer.

"Lord," she prayed, "please use me. Let me make a difference in this world. Show me what You are doing, and allow me to be a part of it. I feel as though I am just waking up to realize how much there is to fight for. Assure me that my work is not yet finished, and allow me to be a tool in Your mighty hand that would impact those around me. Give me purpose, Lord. I want to know that my work is not finished just because the children have grown. I want to reach this lost and hurting world, Father. I want to shine Your light so others might see who You are and how greatly You love them."

A warm and empowering thought filled her mind as she prayed. She recognized that the thought came from God.

Free the captives.

She turned to a fresh page in her journal and wrote the words down as she pondered them out loud.

After a few moments of reflection, she flipped through her journal, as she often did, looking for little reminders of how God had answered her prayers in the past.

> Lord, please be with my girl, Grace. She is struggling to find close friends. The strong ones, that make you stronger. She needs Your guidance as she considers her next steps. College? Career? What would You have for her future, Father? Please reveal it to her in such a clear way that she will see Your hand guiding her. Make the path straight and the darkness light around her.

She had added scripture to that entry:

> I will bring the blind by a way that they knew not; I will lead them in paths that they have not known: I will make darkness light before them, and crooked things straight. These things will I do unto them, and not forsake them. (Isaiah 42:16)

She smiled and took in a deep, cleansing breath. She dwelt on the memory of how God had answered that prayer. The plan that Grace had now as she looked forward to college with a new friend. She took a moment to jot down the story so she could reference it when her faith was weak.

She had learned to do this from her old friend, Mae. They had read in Deuteronomy how the children of Israel stacked stones of remembrance. This prayer journal was her version of the stones—of all that God had done for her. She wrote out her prayers and noted when and how God answered them. While so many prayers had a noted answer, not all of them did—and it was those entries that she would visit and pray over like old stories. She believed that one day each one would have an answer.

Now as she opened her Bible to the chapter she was reading today, she was excited to see what the Lord had to say. She had spent the last few months walking through the book of Isaiah, and today she opened the pages to chapter 61. The words lit a fire in her soul.

"The Spirit of the Lord God is upon me; because the Lord hath anointed me to preach good tidings unto the meek; He hath sent me to bind up the brokenhearted, to proclaim liberty to the captives—"

Goosebumps raised on her arms.

"Yes, Lord!" she exclaimed so loudly that the dog jumped at her feet.

She finished reading the passage: "and the opening of the prison to them that are bound."

"That is exactly what I want to do! Allow me to liberate the captives!"

As she read the verse aloud, she jotted it down in her prayer journal. "Very curious." She spent some time meditating on it, considering the multiple questions that came to her mind and the myriad of thoughts that it stirred.

What captives? Am I to start serving with the prison ministry? Is there someone specific I should meet or connect with? What is a captive? Where should I begin? When do You want me to start?

She wrote them all down. She wrote the verse down in her own words, considering what it meant to her.

Melody dwelled on these words for the rest of her day.

Three

Billy tossed the manila file onto his desk as he grabbed the pot of coffee from the nearby counter. He filled a plain paper cup with the amber brew, mumbling about finding good coffee, and turned back to his desk.

Narrow, uniform desks lined the center of a long, expansive room. File cabinets and countertops ran along the wall that boasted double doors, while windows filled the opposite wall. Billy's desk sat opposite his partner, Russell Dixon. Dixon could have been a model. In fact, he had posed for the police and firefighters' annual calendar for the last three years. His jet black hair had no signs of gray, and he kept it cut clean. His strong and muscular build was evidence of a healthy lifestyle, at least when he was around Billy.

"There's our new case." Billy nodded toward the file as he choked down his lukewarm coffee. His partner picked up the file. Billy filled him in: "Missing kid. Seven-year-old Lily Chamberlain. Dad's been with the Bureau for fifteen years, so no telling how long we will have to work this before they come in."

Dixon looked through the contents of the folder quickly. Billy noticed he pulled at his collar and cleared his throat a few times. His face flushed slightly as he read through the details.

"You okay?" Billy asked, crushing the empty paper cup in his hand, then tossing it into the trash can under his desk. Although they had been partners for the last year, they were a long way from friends. In fact, Billy found that he had a hard time trusting the man. Integrity didn't seem important to Dixon, as Billy had caught many errors in his reporting as well as outright lies. Not enough to require a confrontation, but enough for Billy to remain alert.

"What?" Dixon didn't look up from the file. "Oh, yeah … no, I'm fine. Need some water. Tickle in the throat." He set the file down, made his way to the water cooler, and gulped down three paper cones of water. He crumpled the cups and shot some baskets before returning to the desk.

"So, what's your take?" Dixon asked.

"Well, she was with her family at a park over in Doylestown. The mom says Lily was on the slide but never came down. She was watching from the park bench. Never saw a struggle. Her little sister was fine but didn't see anything happen. Not sure how we're gonna get any leads on this, but we should head over to the park and check it out."

"Yeah, that sounds good." Dixon grabbed his hat from his desk and headed for the door. "I'll drive."

"Sure, man. Right behind you." Billy followed.

Arriving at the park, the two observed the playground from the car before approaching. They didn't want to start a panic. The news had already traveled that the girl was missing. Billy noticed posters stapled to nearly every telephone pole at the park. Several parents were gathered in small circles, some of them pointing to the two detectives.

"Have you found her?" one man asked boldly, stepping into the path of the oncoming detectives. The guy had two small children with him, so Billy assumed he was the dad. But he never worked off an assumption.

"We are working on it." Dixon was brief and curt; he didn't pause to converse with the man, instead brushing past him. "Do you have any information you would like to share?"

The man clammed up and shook his head. He led his boys down the path and left the park. Other parents followed suit. Billy knew there was something about police on the scene that had the ability to make the event more real to people.

One young mom tentatively approached the detectives. Billy guessed she was maybe twenty and had married well, judging by the size of the diamond on her hand. She was pushing a Versace stroller with a large diaper bag hanging off the front handles.

"Hey, I had a sketchy thing happen last week," she offered, her eyes narrowing against the sun.

"Sure." Billy walked over to a bench and offered for her to sit. "I'm Detective Everett, and this is Detective Dixon. What's your name?" He made the introductions while pulling out a notebook and pen.

"I'm gonna take a look around." Dixon strolled away and began to inspect the playground.

The young woman followed Billy to the bench and sat. "Talia Wilson," she stated.

She seemed nervous to Billy, picking at her fingers, and twisting her watch around her wrist. He tried to put her at ease. "Any details you can give us may help us find the little girl. Tell me about what happened." He angled his body to see her more directly as they sat side-by-side on the bench.

A tentative smile formed, and she began to share. "Well, there was this kid, I don't know … maybe ten or eleven. He had tan skin, short, dark hair, and brown eyes. He asked to play with my nephew. My nephew is only five, and that doesn't happen much. Ya know, kids like to play at their level. Like a five-year-old is still a baby when you're eleven." She shrugged her shoulders and rocked the stroller a little as her baby started to fuss.

"Right," Billy agreed.

"So, I was here with my nephew, Rocky. He's headstrong and doesn't really fear much so you really can't take your eyes off him. And this kid comes over and asks if he can play with Rocky. I was all tied up with this little princess." Her smile grew and her eyes were soft when she looked into the carriage. "I said yes, they could play, but they had to stay where I could see them." She turned back to Billy. "I mean, I'm not a helicopter, but you gotta be smart. The world is crazy."

"Very wise." Nodding, Billy paused from his notes to maintain eye contact.

She took a deep breath. "Anyway, this little boy was kind and said his grandma was over in the baby park with his little brother. It's all stuff you see here every day, but something struck me. That mommy radar or whatever. I just didn't trust him all the way …" Her voice trailed off slightly as her gaze returned to the playground. "I still said yes." She shook her head.

"But I watched 'em, and it didn't take long. I saw what this kid was up to. He was playing with Rocky and being really sweet, but he kept moving farther away from me. Then he grabbed Rocky by the wrist. And that is one thing you gotta know about my nephew, he won't do anything he doesn't *want* to do." She laughed a little. "It maybe saved him this time."

Billy's eyes moved to the playground, taking in all of the activity as Talia paused. The swings were full of giggling kids and the center island was bustling with kids climbing up, sliding down, and jumping off all the many ins and outs of the equipment. He watched as Dixon took the steps two at a time. He appeared to be checking something out around the entrance of the yellow slide. His expression was tight, his lips a thin line.

After a few moments of silence, Talia returned to the conversation, and Billy listened, still taking notes.

"I didn't think about reporting it then, he was just a kid, ya know? But after what happened—with that little girl going missing—I know it was a close call for us." Her eyes welled up a bit, and her voice was tight, but she picked up the story. "He was trying to drag Rocky over to the bushes." She pointed a manicured finger, as her bracelets jingled, to the far side of the playground. Bushes lined the edge with a row of trees behind them. "It's just a gravel access road behind there. And it's not really blocked off at the east end—you can get in and out free and clear. My friends and I would go through that way in high school. Easy in. Easy out."

The baby started to cry louder, and she stood up to go, shaking a little.

"I'm sorry," she said, explaining the obvious. "I need to get her home. Time for a nap." She busied herself with the baby.

"What happened with Rocky? He's okay, yes?" Billy directed her back to the story.

"Oh, yeah. He dug his heels into the rubber pellets, and I started screaming at that kid. He looked scared when he realized I saw them. Rocky told me he said he would give him a new puppy and all the candy he wanted, but my nephew is smart. My sister and I ingrained him with stranger danger, and like I said, the kid's a brute. He is solid, and there is no moving him once he makes up his mind. So finally, the boy dropped Rocky's wrist and bolted through the bushes, where I suppose he had planned to take Rocky. I ran back there but didn't see a thing. No vehicle. No tracks. No kid."

Billy thanked her and reassured her that she had done the right thing. "You can always follow your 'mommy radar' in matters like this. It's better for us to have too much information than not enough. Thank you for sharing this with us. Would you be willing to come into the station to make an official statement?"

"Yeah, sure," she said with conviction.

Dixon rejoined his partner. "Nothing out of place here," he said, shrugging.

She started down the path, toward the lot full of parked SUVs and sedans. "Oh, Detective …" Turning back, her eyes sparked with a memory. "There is something else."

"Yes?" Billy had started to put his notebook away but pulled it back out as she spoke.

"There was a tattoo on the back of his neck." Her eyes looked to the right like she was searching for a better word. "A snake eating its own tail." She shrugged and headed to her car.

Billy made note of the details as his mind tried to piece it all together. A kid recruiter or abductor. A brand. He was concerned that this might be more than they thought.

Shifting awkwardly, Dixon began walking back to the car. "Let's get outta here," he suggested without looking back.

"I just want to check one thing out." Billy headed toward the bushes. "You go ahead; I'll catch up in a minute."

Dixon either didn't hear him or chose not to respond, but Billy barely noted it. He crossed to the bushes and pressed through a scraggly row of pine trees with branches that curtained off the access road behind them. Stepping out onto the gravel road, he surveyed the area. Another row of trees lined the far side of the gravel strip, keeping it completely hidden from view. Pine needles gathered along the edges among the rocks. He heard something scurry. His eyes landed on some black strips along the edge of the trees, bordering the road. He walked over to them and picked up the objects, turning them over in his hand.

Zip ties.

Four

Mind fuzzy. Eyes heavy. Head throbbing. Cassie slowly began to awaken to the world around her. She heard men in conversation and felt the thin carpet beneath her. Cassie thought they must be on a highway as she listened to the roar of semi-trucks passing by with the steady, rhythmic hum of the tires. The timing of streetlights allowed her small glimpses into the space around her.

"Ethan said to take them to 49th Street," the driver stated.

Them. She processed that word. The thoughts began somewhere deep in her soul and erupted in her heart. She was not alone. She was not at home. She did not know these men.

"Whatever, man. He's got more than thirty places. I can't keep 'em straight," another man grumbled.

I've been abducted.

The words were hot fire in her mind, both pain-filled and sobering. Paralyzed with shock, she felt the tears slip from her eyes. *Oh God, please help me. Oh, my God.*

The Lord is close to the brokenhearted.

The words formed in her mind, pulled from her memory. Her breathing started to race. Her palms grew clammy. She counted to ten, desperate to stave off the panic. *This can't be happening. It has to be a nightmare.* Her breathing grew more erratic. *Please do not leave me, Father. Please no matter what comes, please be with me. Nothing bad will happen. I'll be saved. Somehow, I have no idea how, but somehow, get me home.*

She drew in a slow, ragged breath and willed the tears to stop. Fighting to stay focused—for fear the terror would win and she would start screaming—she shifted her thoughts to her surroundings. She pressed her hand into the hard, carpeted floor ... maybe a van? There were no seats, which she concluded meant some sort of work van. Then bits and pieces came back—walking the street, seeing the guy with the man-bun, the white van ... So far, she could distinguish just two voices. The streetlights flashing in gave her brief glimpses of lumps of something else in the van with her. Garbage bags, maybe?

The vehicle began to slow, leaning slightly as if they were taking an exit. She felt a stop and then a right turn. In order to give her mind something to do, she began counting the turns and stops. Wondering how many she had missed already, she still hoped for a chance to escape.

Finally, after what seemed no more than fifteen minutes, the van shuddered to a stop. She tried to formulate a plan. She pulled herself into a crouching position, her head throbbing with every move. Then when the door opened, she would bolt past them and run like her life depended on it. She listened as the seatbelts clanked and the door creaked as it opened. A cool breeze swept into the cabin. Much cooler than any she would have felt in Florida.

One of the men grunted as he lifted his body from the seat. Shadows offered partial coverage from her vantage point in the corner farthest from the doors.

In the dim light offered by the dome on the ceiling, she tried to obtain some details. The ceiling was high, with two rear windows on the double doors. *Probably tinted*, she thought.

The carpet under her was old. It smelled musty and dank. She saw blotchy stains of ... something. Blood came to her mind, but she forced that thought out.

The back doors ripped open, making a loud screech. Two more men and one woman had joined the original two. Cassie felt hope flee, and she sank back against the wall of the van. The wall of men convinced her that bolting was not an option. One reached in to grab what Cassie took to be garbage, and she caught the glimpse of a gun at his waist, further convincing her that even if she managed to run, she would not make it far. Yet all of her senses were on high alert as she looked for any opportunity that might be given to escape.

She still did not move a muscle. Directly across from Cassie, one of the lumps began to move. Slowly, Cassie realized this was a young girl—twelve, maybe thirteen—staring straight at her. She was wearing ripped jeans and a loose T-shirt. Her black hair was pulled back in a tight bun and her dark eyes were piercing.

"Don't fight," she whispered fiercely. The guards were deep in conversation as they mapped out their assignments. "They like it when you fight, but you won't like what they do."

Cassie's head was spinning. It all became suddenly clear when the girl spoke. It wasn't a nightmare; it was real. Her body shuddered. She was away from home, away from her family, all because of a fight with her mother. Rage filled her. She was here because they were unreasonable. None of this would have happened if they had just *listened* to her.

A large angry man started shouting. With the words of the girl's warning still in the air, Cassie jumped when the guard began to yell, first in English and then in Spanish. Looking between the men and the girl, she felt frozen with fear. All thoughts of the past evaporated in the intensity of this moment. In a panic, she frantically searched for any way out.

However, in an instant, she knew escape would not come. Or rather, even if it did, she would not take it. To her right, curled up in a tight, tiny little ball, was a little girl. Sitting up in disbelief, Cassie scanned the space and saw the others. In the darkness, she had mistaken them for heaps of trash. Indeed, they had all appeared to be nothing more than balled-up waste. Surely that was how the captors viewed them. Now, in growing horror, she realized they were all children.

How did they manage to capture enough kids to fill the van?

It was beyond her understanding. With her blond hair in knots and tear stains down her ruddy cheeks, the little girl beside Cassie could not have been more than seven years old. The fear in the child's eyes held Cassie in a vise grip.

As her heart sank, a resolve burned deep within her. She looked around the van full of semiconscious children. *How can this happen? Who can stop it? Is there anyone that can rescue us?*

The children who had been sleeping were abruptly woken with a terrified start, and most began to cry. Some seemed to still be in shock. For Cassie, it felt like the beginning of a horrible nightmare. Human trafficking—a reality that existed beneath the fabric of society—had quickly become her living terror. Something horrible that she had heard about, but never questioned. A truth that had just merged with her picturesque life and would alter her forever.

Five

Beth lifted Esther from her car seat and placed her on the cement. She held tightly to the little one's hand while waiting for Maggie to crawl through to meet them. With her purse on her shoulder and a child holding each hand, Beth led the girls into the medical office building. Beth hated to move the girls from their former pediatrics office, but having someone local was important to her. If the girls ever needed to go to the hospital, she wanted their doctor to be able to treat them. So, after some careful research and reading several online reviews, she found a group practice she wanted to try.

"Is there going to be shots, Mama?" Maggie asked, her little face scrunched up.

"Not today, darling. It's just to meet the new doctor," Beth explained with an encouraging squeeze of her hand.

"Will we have to go by ourselves?" Esther asked.

"No, of course not, baby girl. Mommy will be with you the entire time." Beth noticed her little one let go of a deep sigh.

They arrived at the front window, and Beth provided their insurance card and photo ID to the pleasant receptionist and completed several lengthy forms while waiting for the nurse. The dancing cartoons playing on the wall-mounted TV engaged the girls. Beth took time to note the cleanliness of the waiting room. The temperature seemed a bit chilly, but otherwise, the first impression was pretty good.

After a few moments, the secretary called Beth to the window.

"I'm so sorry, Mrs. Everett. Dr. Morrison was called out in an emergency. We can work you into the schedule with Dr. Clark. Would that be okay?"

"Well—" Beth was a little put off, and it showed in her short tone. "I intentionally made the appointment with the medical director, as I wanted to understand a bit about the practice before moving my children here."

"I understand," offered the girl kindly.

Her sincerity swayed Beth. She changed her tone.

"Of course, I guess it says a lot that he is willing and able to change his schedule to accommodate a patient in crisis. Okay, I imagine we will see the other doctors in the practice at some point. Dr. Clark will be fine."

"Great. The nurse will be with you soon, then. Thank you for understanding." With that, she closed the thin glass window between them.

Beth returned to her seat and explained the change to the girls.

"A girl doctor?" Maggie seemed to brighten.

Soon they were in the exam room waiting to meet Dr. Clark. The room was small and white with bright art on one wall. A computer desk with a wheeled stool was just beside the door. A long, cushioned exam table filled the wall opposite the door. It was raised to allow the patient to be at an accessible level for the physician. Maggie used the step stool and climbed up first. Beth lifted Esther and sat her beside her sister.

Without a courtesy knock, the doctor burst through the door. *Strike one,* thought Beth.

A stout, heavyset woman entered the room and seemed to fill the entirety of the small space. Standing in front of the girls, Beth noticed how they both seemed to shrink back against the wall as the doctor began to introduce herself. In response to her girls, Beth felt her mama bear awake.

"Hello, Mrs."—she glanced at the papers—"Everett. I'm Dr. Clark. Thank you for accommodating the schedule change. Sorry about the inconvenience." Her tone was brusque.

Beth held out her hand. "Pleasure to meet you, Dr. Clark."

The doctor reluctantly offered a fist bump and immediately washed her hands.

Beth sent an encouraging smile to her girls. "Well, we are new to the area and are looking for a new pediatric group. Your practice comes highly recommended."

"Yes, we are the premier location in the area."

She sounds smug, Beth thought. But if they were indeed the best practitioners in town, she'd be glad.

"Well, aren't you two so pretty?" The doctor turned her full attention to the girls.

Beth felt as if she had been dismissed yet she did not abandon her position in front of the girls. The girls smiled shyly and ducked behind their mother's shoulder. Dr. Clark reached past Beth's shoulder to brush Esther's wayward strand of hair, and the little one recoiled at her touch. That action drew a frown from the physician, and her eyes narrowed.

"Do you have any questions for me, Mrs. Everett?" Dr. Clark now turned her back to the family and squatted on the stool in front of the computer.

"Umm ... Yes." Beth pulled up the notes she had on her phone. "Is your practice open 365 days of the year?"

"Yes." She did not look up from the computer.

"Great! Will I be able to request a specific doctor for our visits, or is it booked by availability?"

"Technically, both. For a wellness visit, you will be with me, and for the sick visits, with whoever is available."

"Well, just to clarify—" Beth faltered a little; confrontation was hard for her. "I will be able to establish with a physician of my choosing, correct? For the wellness appointments, I mean. I'd like to still meet with Dr. Morrison."

The doctor stopped typing for a moment, hands frozen over the keys. "Of course." She turned slowly to face Beth, her mouth pressed into a thin line, and her tone was tight and short. "We generally have our patients establish their care with the first physician they see, I suppose you can change that."

Beth could tell by the curt tone that she had offended the physician.

"I don't mean any disrespect. I just—"

"I completely understand. If you have no other questions, you can step outside while I examine the children." Dr. Clark was already standing again and approached the girls.

"Oh, well ..." Beth flushed and stood her ground between the doctor and her children. This was not agreeable to her one bit. She held up her hands in a pleading gesture. "No, that's quite all right, Doctor. I am not here for an exam, and neither will I leave the room. At this point, while you wear a white coat, you are still a perfect stranger to me and my girls."

The doctor stepped back abruptly. Her eyes narrowed, and Beth fumbled a bit under the scrutiny.

After a moment, Dr. Clark pulled the office business card from a tray on the small computer desk. She handed it to Beth. "Well, okay. Here is a list of all of our physicians. You can ask any further questions of the front desk staff, and I thank you for choosing our practice." With that, she left the room.

Beth stood dumbfounded, staring out the half-open door. The girls tugged at her hands. "Is that it, Mama?" asked Esther.

"Well, I guess so!"

Beth turned to pick up her bag and help the girls down from the exam table when a nurse knocked softly on the opened door. A tall blonde in her twenties walked into the room.

"Hello," she said with a smile, her tone warm. "I'm so sorry to interrupt, but I am Dr. Morrison's nurse and he asked me to check on his patients and personally apologize for today's scheduling change. How did things go with Dr. Clark?"

Beth was still flushed and growing more furious as she thought through the visit. "Not well at all. That woman was presumptuous and dismissive. If I were to base my decision about choosing this office on the staff, I would say yes. But based on *that* interaction, it would be a resounding no!"

The nurse stood calmly in the face of Beth's tirade. "Mrs. Everett, I cannot say anything outside of my position, but I would sincerely ask that you try again and set an appointment with Dr. Morrison. I am certain that he would be interested in hearing about your experience, as the patient is his primary focus. I know the decision is solely in your court, but if you would offer us another opportunity, I am confident we would exceed your expectations." She handed Beth a flier that detailed all of the practitioners with their thumbprint photo.

Her words melted Beth's anger. "Of course. I am so thankful that you took the time to check on us. I am sorry it was such an unfortunate experience, but I will try again—with Dr. Morrison." Adamantly, she pointed to his image on the flier.

The nurse walked them to the checkout desk. "There will be no charge for today's visit," she explained to the receptionist before leaving. "It was a meet and greet."

She turned to Beth. "I hope we can see you again soon."

Both girls waved to the nurse as she walked away.

At the desk, Beth stood awkwardly waiting for the receptionist when Dr. Clark ambled up to the counter. A file folder she carried spilled its contents onto the desk. Dr. Clark furiously picked up the papers. Beth caught a glimpse of several photographs, all of little girls with blond hair and blue eyes.

A chill ran down her spine.

Billy would say I'm letting my imagination run wild, she thought, tamping down the feeling.

Six

The men were still shouting instructions in a mix of Spanish and English. Cassie sat in stunned silence, immovable.

The girl that offered the warning went first. It didn't seem like this was unfamiliar to her. She sat at the edge of the van door with her hands behind her back. She bowed her head and allowed the men to place a blindfold over her eyes. They were rough, and she flinched when the knot pulled out some of her hair, but she did not cry out.

There must have been fifteen kids in the van. When it was Cassie's turn, she tried to peer out into the world beyond the van, hopeful for clues to where they were. All she saw was an abandoned street at night. Everything one would expect in a dark alley in any city across the country. Large dumpsters, trash pushed along by the breeze, rats scurrying. She could have been anywhere.

Three guards blocked her path, canceling any plans for escape. She took in as many details as she could before it all went dark behind the blindfold. The one placing the covering had a patch over one eye. He was large and formidable. His black hair was shaved so close Cassie could see his scalp. He had a goatee with signs of gray and a tattoo of a snake in a circle, mouth devouring its own tail, on his right forearm.

The guard that led Cassie from the van was a woman. Cassie could barely wrap her mind around this. It seemed so atrocious. She yanked and pulled at Cassie, insisting she needed to walk faster. Her voice was gruff, and she was dressed in combat fatigues. Cassie didn't see a snake tattoo but had noticed several scars on her arms.

A heavyset guard completed the trio. From behind, she heard his harsh voice, as he walked with another victim. Cassie cringed as his voice roared in the night. She heard the kid stumble and the guard curse. It took every bit of Cassie's sense to override her desire to put these guards down. And she really believed she could. But she recognized the panic and remained calm.

"Bring it down, Hector," the woman barked. "Ethan will want them fresh for the first meeting."

Blindfolds were yanked off as the children arrived in a small rectangular room. Makeshift fluorescent lights hung from the ceiling. Their eyes struggled to adjust, and fear consumed them as they were given instructions but still no answers.

"On your knees," the portly guard, Hector, bellowed, causing the younger children to jump. "Hands behind your back. Keep your heads down. No talking."

Guards paced around the children, looming over them. While all the children obeyed the orders, whimpering cries filled Cassie's ears. She was terrified, not knowing what was happening, not knowing what would happen. At fifteen, she had a haunting idea, and it made her stomach churn when she thought of the little ones.

"This is your new life," Hector continued. "You will follow the rules or there will be punishment. No exceptions."

A tear escaped and trailed down Cassie's cheek. She struggled to maintain control over the dam of fear and despair that was threatening to break.

A child down the line could not hold back. Hector bent over the child, his face a flame of anger. As he yelled, spittle sprayed on her cheeks. Her crying intensified with the impact of his screams. Cassie stole a sideways glance. The girl was around fourteen, a big girl with a frizzy mess of curls.

Cassie abruptly returned to her position in response to a blow to the back of her head from a guard behind her. "Eyes down," the guard spat.

Down the row, the guard was yelling, "Stop crying, cow!" He smacked the girl upside the head, and the shock silenced her for the moment. Cassie felt her stomach go queasy at the sound.

One of the boys began to panic. From the corner of her eye, Cassie saw a flurry of movement and heard him curse as he raced for the door. Terrified, she kept her eyes down. She heard a gunshot and she jumped. Followed by the children screaming and a thump as his body hit the floor.

The guards chuckled. "There's always a good example, right, Amber." The tattooed guard sneered, acknowledging his coworker. He turned his attention to the rest of the children, "That is what happens to anyone who thinks they can escape."

Amber laughed and turned back to the captives. "Like he said," she picked up where Hector left off, her voice sharp and shrill, "this is your new life."

Cassie did not cry anymore. Fear fed a dark place in her heart, a place where she was giving darkness space to grow. Anger, shame, and vengeance all converged in a swirling typhoon in her heart.

She vowed to kill them all.

Time passed slowly. Darkness blanketed the children. Cassie studied her surroundings, picking up what she could with eyes that were surprisingly adjusted to the dark. No windows and only one door at the narrow end of the rectangle-shaped room.

Sitting against the cold steel with nothing but the soft whimpers of children and her fury to fill her, Cassie thought of her family. It was a dangerous place to go, but she was unable to shove the thoughts away any longer.

She knew thinking of her parents would not help her out of this. Worse, it made her weak and weepy.

This was their fault. If they hadn't been so stupid strict about the party ... I would never have left.

She groaned in her spirit. She knew they would have no way of knowing where she was. Aside from tracking some turns and stops and a reference to 49th Street—or was it Avenue?—she had no idea where she was.

She tried to figure out how long she had been gone. It was dark when they arrived that evening, but she didn't know how many hours she had been knocked out in the van. She wasn't even sure how many days had passed since they arrived. The chill in the room led her to believe she was somewhere far north of her home in Florida.

Depression and doubt battled in her mind. She knew her mom would start the prayer chain, maybe even before placing the missing person report. She scoffed. Faith died in places like this, but it didn't matter. Emotions could have no bearing here. She wasn't sure that anything could rescue her. A time machine or Iron Man, maybe. Take a ride in the TARDIS or have Iron Man deploy some new contraption directed to attack heavily armed thugs, but avoid young children, with wildly deprecating, sometimes brash commentary.

Or maybe God. Yes, it would take God moving mountains. And in this dark horror in which she found herself, a time machine seemed more likely.

Cassie realized she was absently rubbing her finger while taking in what she could about her new "home." After they arrived, the guards collected all the jewelry, and that included the ring her grandfather had given her last year. A simple gold band engraved with Psalm 17:8. Thinking of him and the promises she made to make him proud, to bring him joy … to save herself for her husband, made fresh tears burn in her eyes. She ran through all the possible emotions: Anger. Fear. Despair. Now she settled into resolve, and the burning of those tears enforced her will to escape. Terror threatened to consume her. Still, she refused to think about the reasons *why* she was taken.

Looking to her left she noticed the girl from the van. Walking over, Cassie watched as she pulled her hairband and readjusted her bun. Cassie settled in against the wall next to her, resting her arms against her knees.

"How are you holding up?" she asked softly.

"I don't know." Now the girl fidgeted with her shirt sleeve. "How do you have words for this?"

"That's truth," Cassie agreed. "I'm Cassie." She didn't offer a hand, just stated it as a fact. They sat next to one another, staring into the darkness as they leaned against the cold wall.

"Missy" was all she offered.

"Do you have any idea …" Cassie allowed the sentence to trail off, not sure she was ready for the answer. Not even certain of the question.

"Where we are? What we are here for? What will happen next?" Missy listed the questions off like bullets from a gun. "I have ideas. I've lived through some of it before. This is just my first time with a family."

"A … family?" The word did not fit into any concept Cassie had of family.

With her brows down over her dark eyes, Missy responded in a curt, unfeeling tone. "Sex. We are here for sex, and you might as well get used to it."

Cassie recoiled at the words. Every terrible thought she had banished from her mind flooded her now. Her fears were confirmed in a word. *Sex.* She gasped, and dread took hold of her heart as she processed this new truth. "But … they're *little*. And I … I haven't even—"

"Oh … No. Oh, crap." A broad grin split Missy's face.

Cassie shifted uncomfortably under Missy's gaze.

"You're a virgin." Missy actually laughed. "You'll be worth a fortune."

Breath-catching sobs came from Cassie's core as she doubled over. The enormity of her situation flooded her. She broke. The dam let loose, and tears poured freely. Panic, thick and powerful, started to close her throat. She coughed. She heaved. Missy slapped her back. There was an odd sort of smile on her face.

"I-I can't do this." Cassie's voice dripped with terror, and her eyes were wide.

"Listen. You will *probably* survive." Missy paused, her tone callous and unfeeling. There were moments Cassie thought this girl to be a friend of sorts, and then there were moments like this—when she wasn't fully convinced Missy was human at all.

"At least for a while." Missy continued, "I've lived in places like this since I was nine. I know I'm an exception to the rule, but I'm still breathing." She took Cassie's face in her hands and turned it to her. "Maybe you will too!"

Missy got up then, walked to the other side of the narrow room, and sat down against the wall. One little girl snuggled into her lap, and Missy ran her slender fingers through the child's silky curls. Leaning her head back against the steel, Missy proceeded to fall asleep.

Cassie stared in disbelief, silent sobs wracking her.

How would she survive this? How would these children endure? Good God, how did this even exist? She looked with new eyes at the huddled masses of minors around the room. Driven to prayer, as there was nowhere else to turn, her body shook as she silently stormed the gates of heaven. Her mind raced with unbidden thoughts that she attempted to battle with prayer—until her body fell exhausted onto the steel floor and she slept.

Seven

Cassie began to realize she was part of an ongoing supply of children. The night she and the others arrived, the rectangle room had been empty. Since then, more kids came into the darkness two or three times a day. The overhead fluorescent lights would buzz and flicker for a few moments when the guards came in to drop off their bounty. Their faces reflected fear and shock; Cassie tried to connect with them as quickly as possible.

When a fourteen-year-old girl—who couldn't stop crying—arrived, Cassie attempted to calm her. Dust mixed with tears and snot, leaving dirty streaks down her round dark face that dried on her cheeks. Her curly black hair grew more disheveled every time she ran her hands through it, turning it into a fuzzy cloud over her head. She sat away from the rest of the children and just sobbed. After the guards left and the lights were out, Cassie crawled over to her in the dark room.

She wore an oversized cream sweater that fell off her shoulder, exposing her bra strap. Cassie supposed she had thought that looked sexy when she dressed in her bedroom. The once clean, soft cotton blend was now dirty and snagged from her ordeal. Upon her arrival, she had fought to maintain a ladylike position with her tight miniskirt but had long since given up the attempt in the hours that had passed. She finally opted to sit and crisscrossed her legs, with her tall brown boots covering most of her calves and not much else.

"Hey, what's your name?" Cassie asked, trying to place an arm over her shoulder.

The girl shifted and pulled away sharply. "Leave me alone!" she moaned loudly, pushing Cassie's hand away.

Cassie tried to tell her to quiet down. The guards would come.

"No!" she bellowed. "No, I can't be here. I want my mom … We got into a fight. I was so mad … I want to go back." She continued to wail.

Cassie inhaled sharply, and her hands began to tremble. The memories of her own mother flooded in. Hurrying back to her space, she felt the familiar panic return. She felt a tremor in her hands. Leaning against the steel wall, she needed the cold to keep her tethered to the present.

And just as she had predicted, the guards busted in with threats of what would happen if anyone continued to make noise. The girl recoiled and screamed as they entered. So Melvin the guard, kicked her in the side to emphasize his point. She simpered, curling into a ball on the floor, babbling softly about nightmares and needing to wake up.

Back with her small tribe, Cassie fought to calm herself. Exposed to more base depravity than she ever imagined possible, she was nearly broken. *Mom, if I could just be home with you for five minutes. I'd pray you would never let me go. I would never run away. I'm here and I'm scared and you're there. I know you must be wrecked with grief. What I would give to turn back time, to make different choices. Oh God, help me.*

She forced her attention on these little children. Her purpose. They were what kept her grounded—focused. She was dedicated to finding a way out. She held Lily in her lap as Anna snuggled beside her. She vowed to never stop fighting.

Slowly, the new girl made her way across the room. After accidentally stepping on a few legs and feet in the foreign dark room, she plopped down beside Cassie. She was silent for a few moments, picking at her fingers. Cassie gave her space. There was no easy transition into this terrifying reality.

"Jazmin," she said softly, her breath still ragged and uneven.

"I'm Cassie."

"W-what happens now?" she asked with a tremor in her voice.

"It's not easy." Cassie attempted to soften the blow. "They use us ... for sex." Cassie's voice broke slightly as she was still processing her first experience, which had been followed by several others over the last few days.

The girl bent over, head to knees as she processed, fresh tears flowing with painful sobs.

Cassie placed a hand on Jazmin's back. She didn't react this time. "You must be quiet. They don't get mad if we whisper, but ... you've already seen what they do if we are loud."

Sitting up, Jazmin took several deep breaths through her broad nose and released them long and slow through her mouth. "How do you do this? Why don't you fight? There are a lot of us ... at least thirty. They want us quiet, right? That must mean *someone* can hear us if we're loud. We must get loud!" Her voice a rising crescendo as she spoke.

"Calm down! That is desperation speaking, Jazmin. They have guns—there is only one entrance. I've seen them kill without an ounce of hesitation ... or remorse. It's futile for now. But God will make a way."

Cassie realized she finally believed the words that she spoke.

Both girls jumped when the metal door screeched on its hinges. *We weren't loud,* Cassie thought. But then the overhead fluorescents popped on with their familiar buzzing. Four guards came in, and Cassie knew that meant clients would be arriving.

Melvin came in first with the newest guard. They hadn't learned his name yet, but Cassie named him Stache for the large mustache that lay over his lip like a small rat. The two men moved to the right of the room. Amber and Hector sauntered in behind them.

A young man, with a pronounced limp, hobbled in next. One foot dragged as he walked, he moved slowly and quietly to the far left corner and disappeared into the shadows. Cassie guessed he must be close to thirty. Other than his limp, he was unremarkable. She wasn't surprised he was able to melt into the wall.

Stache started to laugh, nodding his head in the young man's direction and talking too loudly. Cassie was used to them talking as though they were not there, but she watched Melvin as he reacted to the obtuse man. She had learned to read the guards and knew this new guy was making trouble for himself. "What's his deal, man? That the boss's brother?"

Cassie watched the man in the corner. He stared at the guard but said nothing.

Melvin stiffened, eyes facing forward, and told him to shut it, but Stache didn't listen.

"His limp, though. I heard he was an idiot." He thumped Melvin on the arm. "Like, the mentality of a six-year-old. Broke a wall with his head as a kid." Still laughing when the man named Ethan Walker entered the room. Cassie thought of the first time she saw him, on the street the night he gave his men instructions to take her. Hate filled her. Melvin withdrew from Stache quickly, moving to join the other guards.

Without looking at the guards, Ethan approached his brother. Cassie had seen them before, here in this place. She had witnessed their odd relationship—Ethan a caregiver of sorts, James a child of sorts. Placing a hand on his shoulder he said, "James, you can't let anyone ridicule you. No one has the right to mock you. If they laugh at you, they are laughing at me. You don't want to bring shame to me, do you?"

"N-no, Ethan. You're my brother. You're my blood. We protect each other. I will never let you down." James hung his head and clasped his hands together.

Listening to this conversation, the guard began to sputter out an apology. "M-man, I was just teasin'. I didn't mean anything by it, you know."

"Al, why were you mocking my brother?" Ethan's tone was cold but steady. Without turning, he rolled up his sleeves as he spoke.

"No, listen." Al threw his hands up in defense and ambled toward Ethan. "I was just playin'."

James attempted to intervene. "It's okay, Ethan."

Ethan lifted hard eyes to his brother. "If you say it's okay, James, they think they can do it. You have to stand up for yourself, brother. But until you do—"

Without warning, Ethan punched the guard across the jaw and back around to his right eye. He grabbed the pistol from inside his vest and brought the handle crashing down on the man's head. Al fell to the floor, and Ethan directed the other guards to drag him out.

As the men left, another man entered the space. He was tall and well dressed. His silver-gray hair was parted to one side, and his penetrating black eyes assessed the situation.

As Ethan was fixing his sleeve, Cassie gasped when she recognized the mark on his right arm. She instinctively touched her own arm—the same symbol. Realization dawned on her that he had been on this side of the business once. The brand was a marker for anyone who had tried to escape.

She remembered the night she had earned hers. It was an opportunity she couldn't resist, or maybe the panic pushed her beyond reason. She couldn't be sure. She was out with a john, and he was careless. He had just finished with her and had gone into the bathroom. That is when she ran from the hotel room, half-naked and terrified. She made it to the corner store and was flooded with relief when she saw the two cops inside.

"You've got to help me," she cried. Tears splashed down her face as the hope of freedom filled her heart. "I've been abducted! I can tell you everything. Please help me. I'm from Florida." Slowly she began to realize how things looked. "Listen, I didn't run away," She tried adjusting her shirt, fully conscious she had no shoes and could not cover all her shame with the thin material.

The first cop, in his forties, with a bushy unibrow, put an arm around her. "Just calm down, little lady. We will get this all sorted out. You just come with us." He ran a finger softly down the side of her face, placing a wayward strand of hair behind her ear. Cassie's heart skipped a beat when she saw the look that passed between the two men. She forced herself to calm down.

"Yeah, yeah, I'll come with you." She said her voice just a whisper. Her body assumed the position she had been taught—head down, shoulders slumped, no eye contact.

"Good girl," the other man cooed. Her skin crawled.

In the backseat of the police cruiser, locked doors preventing further escape, Cassie withered, and hope left her a deflated balloon. "Hey, Ethan," Unibrow spoke into his phone. "We have one of your girls."

A small prickle began on the back of her neck and trailed down her spine, pulling her from the dark memory. James had stepped out of the shadow and was staring directly at her. The attention made her nervous. He wiped saliva from the side of his mouth with his shirt sleeve. When she caught his eye, his smile broadened, and he waved at her. She shuddered.

Cassie was snapped out of her memory.

"Line up," Ethan demanded. If he had noticed the exchange between his property and his brother, Cassie didn't see it.

The children moved fast because they knew what would happen if they didn't. As the kids formed a roughly straight double line with the taller kids in the back and the shorter ones in the front, Cassie cringed as she likened it to a sick version of a school class photo. It also put the most vulnerable as first picks. Her stomach churned.

Ethan pointed to Jazmin. Cassie stood frozen. Jazmin, head down, was taking ragged breaths as new tears formed. She was opening and closing her hands in rapid movements … panic rising. The guards came, pulled her out of the line, and stood an arm's length on either side of her.

"There are certain expectations that we need to meet," the new man began dryly as if addressing a nine a.m. department staff meeting. "Ethan has taught you about our criteria, our rules … Look good. Be good. And we don't ever—"

"Talk to anyone," all the children echoed in a unison response.

"That's right." A slow smile spread across his face, revealing perfectly shaped teeth. "Today, one of you is not up to my standards." With one gesture, the guards took Jazmin by both arms. She kicked and thrashed and moaned. As they hauled the round-faced girl from the room, she just howled harder, melting into pleas to let her go. It took both guards to lead her toward the door. Her body flailed, then she apparently tried to go limp.

Finally, a hard smack across the face brought her hysterics to a simmer and she obeyed their directives, though her tears never subsided. Her head wobbled strangely as she was half-led, half-dragged from the room.

Cassie believed some kids were brought in just to be used as examples to hold the rest of them in fear. Fear made them so much easier to control.

Finding herself somewhat numb to the tears was a slow realization that made Cassie sad.

In the aftermath of Jazmin's removal, James shuffled over to his brother. Without any reservation, he pointed at Cassie directly. He kept hungry eyes on her during the entire conversation with his brother.

She fidgeted with her fingers, uncomfortable with their direct attention. Finally, shoving her hands at her side, she willed her body to be still. She did not want to provide them with any insight into her state of mind. There was so little she could control; she held fast to that.

Ethan listened without looking at his brother. Cassie watched as his face turned to stone, and his mouth became a thin, tight line. He held his hand up and silenced his brother's words. "We've discussed the girls, James. They are off limits to you."

The tall man interjected himself into their conversation. "Ethan, do we have a problem?"

Ethan didn't even turn as he replied, "No, Draven. My brother is my business. You have nothing to do with him."

"I would remind you that anything that interrupts *this* business will become *my* business." Draven's tone was menacing.

Cassie steamed, and James pouted. He obediently tottered back to his corner. Her cheeks flushed at the reminder that she was a bought-and-paid-for commodity. Even as the thought was on her mind, the first client of the night slithered through the door.

Eight

Melody pushed the grocery cart absently as she checked items off her list. She barely took in her surroundings: Bread—aisle three. Canned goods—aisle seven. She was familiar enough with the store to navigate each aisle and know which items she would find. Robotically, she maneuvered the cart around each corner.

About a year ago, the store had been rearranged, and it had taken her a good three months to learn the new pattern, but now it was old hat yet again. Sometimes she felt like that was her life. All the same stuff, all the same aisles—row after row of knowing exactly what to expect.

Now, she felt a low coming on. She longed for some adventure in life.

She turned the corner of aisle four to nearly run over a young girl in pigtails. She stopped and quickly pulled the cart back. The end display of cereal boxes went flying as her cart made abrupt contact.

"Oh, whoa!" she exclaimed, smiling. "Esther Everett?" Melody thought the Everett family lived on the other side of town.

Esther had started picking up the boxes when her mom appeared and immediately began to help her. Without looking up, Beth began offering a profuse apology and wearing a look of exasperation. "Esther, please don't run off!" Her attention focused on her youngest, while the older girl kept her hand dutifully on the cart.

Then she turned to address Melody. "I am so sorry my daughter caused this!"

Esther pointed at Melody and asked without embarrassment, "Isn't she from church, Mama?"

Recognition dawned in Beth's eyes when she finally looked up at who her child had run into. Standing up and brushing her knees, Beth smiled at her old friend. "Melody Rey! How nice to see you! I had no idea this was your store!" Her smile was bright and broad. "I am so glad it's you!" She laughed and went on, "I mean, an old friend and not a cranky stranger!"

Melody laughed. "It is funny how we claim the stores closest to us! What brings you here? Aside from cereal and ketchup."

Instantly, memories of all the wonderful conversations they'd had while serving together at their church filled Melody's mind. Beth had just been getting into homeschooling, and Esther was ... two or three, Melody couldn't remember exactly. Happy to guide her with numerous insightful mommy lessons—both good and bad—Melody had spent many services with Beth, burping babies and sharing stories. She hoped her bits of wit and wisdom had helped Beth through some challenging times, with Esther in particular. It struck Melody when she realized their relationship had not developed outside of the infant room. Such was life with so many moving parts. It was difficult to make friendships and even more so to maintain them.

"Oh, we moved this way about two months ago. The girls are getting bigger, and the two bedrooms weren't working for us anymore, plus they just needed space to run! The Lord blessed us with a great house with more space and a beautiful backyard. I needed somewhere that these two could exert some energy. Homeschooling them is a blessing, but it is a *lot* of work!"

She laughed easily, yet Melody could sense the stress she was carrying. She remembered the prayer chain when the tragedy had hit the young family. She had spent many days in prayer for her friend. While she was in a new season herself with her two boys basically on their own and her daughter heading into her senior year of high school, she easily recalled the struggle of the season when they were all home, all underfoot, and at times, all presenting unique challenges.

"Listen, I would love to reconnect!" Melody offered. "I could take you for coffee and we can find a place with a playground. The girls can play, and we can chat."

Beth noticeably brightened at the thought. "That would be amazing! Just some adult conversation would be thrilling at this point!"

Both ladies laughed. They shared their numbers and parted to finish their shopping. Melody smiled and waved at Esther, who lagged behind, swinging her arms, and smiling at her mom's friend. Then she heard her mother calling her and she bolted. Melody chuckled and finished finding the items on her list.

On Monday, Beth and Melody met for an early lunch at a restaurant with a play place. When Beth arrived, breathless, hustling the girls and late as usual, she placed the order at the counter and sought out Melody. She found her at a table near the glass-enclosed playground.

That was thoughtful, Beth thought.

The girls quickly finished their meals of chicken and french fries, while Melody and Beth engaged in small talk. Once the girls were freed to go play, the women were equally free to talk about weightier matters with minimal interruption.

Beth took feverish notes while Melody shared some of her homeschool tips and tricks. Melody shared freely and the conversation flowed organically from topic to topic. Beth was tiptoeing around the burden she had been carrying, really hoping that Melody would be able to help.

"What is it, Beth?" Melody gently asked when Beth had paused.

Beth took a deep breath and began. "It's this dark world, Melody. It's seeing my girls and reading headlines of horror and knowing that they'll have to face all of this, sooner than I would like. And how on earth am I going to protect them? Human trafficking is a hub here. With the interstate providing easy access to several other states and some shady politicians, judges, and you know … It all seems to be so put together and impossible to take back apart. That massage parlor was just shut down, and it turned out the owner was using it to traffic underage girls. And the ring was led by a woman! We can't even protect our own! Then there are billionaires like Draven Wolfe funding goodness knows what kind of evil ... I'm just living each day feeling terrified for my children and asking God, 'What can I do?'"

"I get it, Beth. I really do. Grace is out there in this mess too. She's older and I've equipped her enough to be safe, but not filled with fear. The first thing to know is the facts. You should do more research on how to identify trafficked victims and how to protect yourself, and your daughters, from becoming one. And don't read so many headlines."

Beth blanched a little at that and wondered how Melody could have known she was a headline skimmer.

Melody didn't seem to notice. "The Bible tells us to take every thought captive." She picked up her cup but continued before taking a drink. "That will be a lot easier if you are filtering and deciding what you want to allow to influence those thoughts. Are you reading some slanted journalist's opinion piece or something that will provide you with wisdom and understanding?" She reached across the table to give her friend an encouraging pat on the hand. "If you continue to fill your mind with our current news reports, you will live in defeat." She took a drink of soda.

Beth smiled. Maybe she had noticed her reaction.

Melody continued. "You need to fill your mind with the Word of God and then do some research. As ridiculous as it might sound, I've found some grassroots reporters who I trust—on social media, of all places. There are so many stories, all on what we would consider reputable news sources, that are just bought-and-paid-for propaganda.

"And what people once called conspiracy theories are starting to come to light. Like Project Mockingbird, where the CIA has commissioned agents to be news reporters. Couple that with the fact that one of our previous presidents signed an executive order that repealed the propaganda ban and now the 'government-made news'—" She used air quotes and a perfect eye roll to emphasize what she thought of that. "—is being spread to Americans every day like it's gospel truth. It is dark, and sadly, the world will become darker before Jesus calls us home. But we're close! Lord Almighty, we *must* be close!" She smacked the table for emphasis.

Beth nodded in agreement. "Lord, I hope so." She quietly mumbled as she jotted down the details she wanted to research further. "I am going to do some research tonight. But first, the Bible. Honestly, I had not realized until this moment how consumed I have become with the negative state of this world. From the latest rumors of plans for another pandemic to wars, and human trafficking … well, it's been hours of surfing. I just have had a hunger to learn more. But I know I have let my time in the Word slip. Considerably. That has to change." Her tone reverberated with her commitment.

It was time for Beth to leave so she could finish up her afternoon of lessons with the girls. She stood and gave Melody a hug and a sincere thank-you. "It would be so great if we could meet again sometime. I can't tell you what these couple of hours have meant to me. I appreciate you so much!"

"I was thinking about starting a new Bible study." Melody turned to grab her purse. "My friend Mae Murphy and I try to meet a couple of times a month. Would that interest you?" Melody offered.

"Yes!" Beth nodded emphatically. "Adult time and Bible study. I'm down!" She laughed.

Pulling out their phones, they secured a date for the following week. Beth had learned that if she wanted to do something, it had to be on the calendar.

The girls were now hanging onto Beth's arms. "Apparently, they are ready for school." She smiled down at the girls as she turned from her friend.

"No!" They cried in unison, but Beth moved them along, and they were on their way. She was already looking forward to next week.

Nine

Cassie quickly learned their job was to make the customers happy; do whatever they asked. Thinking of the things she was forced to do, and considering the children around her, the familiar fire of rage burned her soul.

While she often dreamed of escape, she was not able to see a way out. It was a tight chamber and constantly guarded. It reminded her of a dank and musty locker room after football practice. There was a makeshift shower at the far end of the room. There was no curtain—she supposed livestock didn't need privacy. A Porta Potty ensured a constant offensive odor permeated the room. They replaced it weekly, but that did not make a difference.

One girl had tried to escape by hiding in the pit. The moment when they dumped her out, and the contents along with her, was burned in Cassie's mind. The smell came back with the memory, and she gagged a little.

The girl didn't live to remember it.

Hard, frigid steel surrounded the children—the floor, the walls, the ceiling. With no provision of covers or cushions, the bitter cold seeped into their bodies. Snuggling together in groups of four or five offered some success in capturing both warmth and comfort. All of them feared the opening of the door and clients arriving.

Her first experience had been a terror she would never forget. She was selected by a soft, overweight, middle-aged man with gapped teeth, large canines, and bad breath. Saliva trickled from his open mouth to his ratty beard. He was jittery, bouncing back and forth on his feet. Cassie was repulsed. To herself, she named him Wolfman.

Fields of Gomorrah

After being taken to the back alley she had come through the night of her arrival, Cassie had been blindfolded and led into the back seat of a limo. Wolfman laughed, low and evil, when she asked to remove the blindfold. In the next instant, he was on top of her, all tongue and teeth. She forced herself to quell the fear and relax her fists. She had nowhere to run, and this foul man was no hero.

Arriving at a seedy motel—Cassie assumed it was all he could afford after paying for her services—he dragged her out of the back seat into the shadow of night. He grabbed a small black case that she had not noticed until that moment.

Wolfman fumbled with the key card, dropped it, mumbled something unintelligible, bent to pick it up, and started again. Cassie felt her stomach churning. Felt the rage growing. Beginning to feel cocky—how easily she could take this guy out—she remembered that fear makes you do stupid things.

Inside, the room smelled of mildew. Cassie did not want to think of what action that saggy bed had seen and even less of what was about to happen. That was when he started talking while opening the black case to an arrangement of small whips and … other things. He gave her detailed instructions for what he wanted her to do. If she took too long, she felt the whip. If she was too quick, she felt the whip. If he just felt like it, she felt the whip. Across her back, her bottom, her face. He laughed with every blow. She imagined what she would do with the whip.

"Call me 'Daddy,'" he whimpered as he pulled her on top of him. His eyes closed as he caressed her exposed skin.

She was silent.

He said it again, more loudly. Still, she ignored the request.

Stopping and grabbing her by the shoulders, he sank thick fingers into her flesh. "I said to call me Daddy."

A spray of spittle accosted her face.

"Are you serious?" She couldn't take it. She couldn't just take it.

A twisted smile slowly blossomed across his face, revealing those crooked teeth, and his eyes narrowed sharply. With a sharp blow to the side of her head, he showed her how serious he was.

"Yes, I'm serious!" He was red-faced now, screeching all his commands like a crow. With short bursts of speech he took what he paid for and left her lying in the bed with the welts and bruises as her only company.

He showered, singing some '70s rock songs, while she wept. He brought her a bag of ice when he was all cleaned up.

Satisfied and feeling jovial now, Wolfman took her to a fast-food joint to buy her ice cream, crooning his appreciation and praising her for being such a good girl. The shift frightened Cassie even more than the crimson maniac she had just seen.

The limo was gone, and in its place was an old beater. It was hard to tell in the motel parking lot lighting, but it was red once, now faded, bent, and scarred. She knew how it felt.

SC19678. She would remember the license plate.

She settled into the front seat, scooting as far away from him as she could. He reached over and smacked her leg and cackled. The shoes she had been given were causing blisters. She slipped them off and they landed in a pile of newspaper and Styrofoam cups. They pulled up to the drive-through.

"Well ..." He finished his sentence with a curse. "It's broken. I know there were some rules..." He looked out the window, sucked air through the gap in his teeth, then turned to Cassie. "I really want ice cream. I guess we'll have to go inside." He brushed her hair from her face and she recoiled, cringing. "You'll be a good girl?" It was posed as a question, but Cassie knew it was a command.

"Of course, Daddy." She shifted the bag of ice on her temple, the lesson still fresh. A broad, crooked smile was his response.

He took the bag of ice from her and pulled her hair over the bruising. "You keep that covered so no one thinks anything is out of place, you got it?"

Despite her desperation, to make contact with anyone other than the handler meant punishment and pain. No one ever escaped. That had been made clear her first night.

Cassie couldn't believe how blind the general public was until now. How they could explain away a dirty child in inappropriate clothes, or worse, not see them at all, made her heart fail.

Standing in line inside the restaurant, he asked, "What would you like, sweetheart?" He whispered in her ear, placing his hand on the small of her back.

He evidently hadn't yet noticed she was barefoot. As they waited, a gaggle of high school boys entered. Harassing each other, insulting each other—normal guy stuff.

For a moment, it seemed like one of them might have seen her. He looked *at* Cassie anyway, not past her like the others. But he just sized her up, pausing at her eyes and landing on her feet. When he raised his eyes in confusion, she held his gaze—first mistake. Smiled—second mistake—and shrugged her shoulders as if to say, *Oh, it's all good. Nothing to see here, buddy. Just left my flips in the car.*

That was the mistake that got her. The actual interaction. She might as well have held out her hand and said, "How do you do? The name is Cassie Woods. Think you could help me out of a jam? You see, I've been abducted recently. Think you could call my mom?"

The attention from the young man infuriated and threatened her own Lothario. The old man took Cassie's wrist in a vise grip; the tight pressure threatened to break the bone. She immediately dropped her eyes, bowed her head, and assumed the acceptable position.

But the damage had been done.

They left the restaurant immediately. She saw the young man staring at her in the reflection of the glass doors as her buyer pushed her through, using her body to open the door for himself. After throwing her into the car, he climbed into his seat and fumbled to get the key in the ignition.

Cassie's body pressed into the seat, trying to avoid the sideways blows. But in his anger, he had failed to reset the blindfold and she took in as many flashing details as she possibly could. Pizza parlors, drugstores; the city streets were lined with businesses of every sort. Street names flew by. She repeated them like mantras in her mind as her body became the punching bag of a maniac. Church. Woodland. Sixty-sixth Avenue. Panda's Pizza. Rite Now Drugs.

When he took a sharp turn into the parking lot, she was able to see her current lodging. Hiding behind an old, abandoned movie theater was a shipping container. A long metal rectangle. It made perfect sense.

The car screamed around the back of the lot, then shuddered to a stop. He got out, still bellowing. The guards came running to see what happened. Amber's face was mottled and blotched as the words came flying from her mouth. "How dare you bring her back like this?"

Cassie knew Amber was only concerned about the merchandise aspect. She had made it crystal clear how she felt about the business: the kids were stock and supplies, nothing more. Her next paycheck. Now, seeing an item returned in Cassie's state meant her pay would be docked.

"She made contact" was all he said, and that was enough to stop Amber cold.

She turned on Cassie and smacked her across the face. Cassie cried out. Amber was much stronger than the man. The man turned and scrambled back into his car.

Amber grabbed her by the hair and dragged her into the rectangle room. Wolfman's taillights were already hitting the street.

Amber held the phone to her ear; Cassie's scalp was on fire.

"One made contact," Amber said through clenched teeth, her grip tightening in Cassie's hair.

Cassie struggled to choke back tears against the pain.

Amber threw her against the wall. "He'll be here to deal with you soon" was her cryptic message.

She stormed out of the room. Missy was the only one who came to Cassie's side. Cassie placed her head in Missy's lap and wept. Fear stole into every part of her.

Later that night, Ethan Walker arrived, wearing a grim expression that chilled Cassie. Amber brought in a kitchen chair and set it in the middle of the room. Melvin and Hector forced Cassie into the chair and held her down after tying her hands behind the back of the chair. All the children were forced to watch as Cassie was made an example.

Ethan took her right foot in his hand. He caressed the raw and blistered flesh from heel to toe. If not for the terror, it would have tickled. He seemed to struggle with the decision of what he was about to do. He shook his head.

"Cassie." Disappointment filled his tone. "Why would you do this? You know the rules." He looked at her expectantly.

Obediently, she responded: "Look good. Obey. Don't talk to anyone."

Her eyes were blinded by tears. She looked wildly around the room, clueless as to what the punishment would be until her eyes landed on a small item in the corner. A typical iron, the kind her mom used to remove the wrinkles from her dad's work clothes. The small, red light seemed like a beacon, despite the blaring light of the bulbs above her. Breathing seemed difficult; she gasped for air as panic flooded her mind. One of the guards placed a dirty rag in her mouth to muffle the cries.

As the hot tip of the iron pressed into the flesh of her foot, screams were muffled by the dirty rag coupled with tears that cascaded down her face as the pain flooded her system. Her eyes were wide with horror. The smell of burning flesh stung her nose. Her flesh. She would never forget that smell. It would take at least a week before she could walk without pain. She'd still have to work, but never again would she forget to slip her shoes back on.

The guards dragged Cassie back to the wall and flung her down. Amber tended to the burn with ointment to clean it, but nothing to alleviate the pain. "Stupid pig," she mumbled coarsely. "They're simple rules. Follow them."

Ethan stood over Cassie. "I do hope you learn your lesson tonight. You have a lot of fire, but you need to tame it. You won't last if you continue to bring me trouble." His eyes were dark, and his voice was tense.

Cassie could only whimper in her pain and terror.

After Ethan and the guards left, Missy came to Cassie and held her until she fell into a fitful slumber.

Ten

Billy sat in his gunmetal gray Dodge Charger. In response to the alert from a text, he glanced at his watch. Dixon was looking for him. He ignored the request and turned his attention to the park.

From his vantage point, he could see most of the playground, the grassy field beside it, and the row of trees he had crossed through just days before. He watched the families that came and went. Most stayed for just under an hour. He noticed there were more dads today … Saturday … presumably giving Mom a few moments of peace.

His watch buzzed against his wrist again. Dixon. Billy dismissed it again. He wasn't ready to address the red flags he was finding about his partner.

At least thirty different family groups had come and gone in the four hours that he had observed. There were parks across the city and even more throughout the county. He shuddered and shifted in the driver's seat when he thought of Beth bringing the girls to the park. It wasn't out of the norm, but now it carried a threat.

Billy shook his head, expecting the physical action to provide some sense of clarity. He would not stay in a place of fear. He turned his attention back to the slides, swings, and teeter-totters.

He focused on the surrounding areas. Talia, the mom he'd met the last time he was here, was very astute. The access road behind this space was an easy thoroughfare for those with nefarious plans. He didn't know what he expected to find today but felt compelled to observe. He mapped out every entrance and exit and concluded that Talia had been spot-on in her assessment.

But it was the boy that weighed on his mind. In his position, he knew that kids recruiting kids was a common practice. But for a child to try to abduct another, on the playground, in plain sight. The gut feeling inside Billy began gnawing at him. He felt certain that this was bigger than he was seeing.

The watch alerted him again. This time he picked up his phone. Dixon had texted twice, and now he was calling. Billy sighed and selected the phone icon to accept the call.

"Yeah," he said into the phone, eyes still on the park.

"I've been trying to reach you." Dixon sounded perturbed.

"Yeah, you've got me," Billy replied, unaffected by the man's curt tone.

"Where are you?" Dixon demanded. There was a lot of shouting and music from Dixon's line.

"It's my day off. Why are you asking?" Billy returned. "Where are you anyway? It's loud."

"I'm … I'm just at the mall, with my kid," he explained, stumbling over his words.

Sounds made up. "Okay, well, did you want something?" Billy asked, growing impatient.

"Just wanted to ask if you found anything more on the case. I've got nothing but dead ends. You have any luck? Maybe we should just make the report and turn it in. This is a waste of time if you ask me." The noise increased on Dixon's end.

"No, man. Nothing yet." For some reason, call it intuition, Billy had not shared the discovery of the zip ties with Dixon. Something about the way the man had been acting bothered him. He couldn't put a finger on it, but it wasn't the first time he felt he couldn't trust his partner.

"But I'm not ready to wrap it up yet. I gotta run. Beth is expecting me by one." He hung up the phone, cutting off Dixon's demands.

He climbed out of the car and strolled over to the playground. He was in plain clothes today, a gray T-shirt and blue jeans. Just a dad scoping out a park for his kids.

"Hello." He greeted the younger dad with a friendly nod. Walking over to the slide, he thought of how that was Lily's last location. He wondered what had happened and how the abduction had transpired. He climbed the steps and ducked down to fit under the overhead covering. He knelt on the platform and leaned against the blue steel wall behind him.

Two boys ran past Billy, laughter trailing behind them. *All children should be free to live without this threat.* He was frustrated. How would he find any leads on this case? He stood to go when an image caught his eye.

He rubbed his thumb across something rough on the side of the yellow plastic slide. A carving. Several carvings … had to be nearly sixty. All were scratched in varying sizes. Billy drew closer to one of the larger images, which was drawn in a childlike fashion. He noted a star with a snake eating its tail in the center. He pulled his phone from his inner jacket pocket and snapped a picture.

This was definitely something. Dixon hadn't mentioned this, he noted to himself as he got up to leave.

Eleven

Cassie heard the argument moments before the men entered the room.

"This is not the business I run, Draven."

She recognized Ethan's voice as he opened the door. Draven walked in with him. The man's face was impossible to read, a mask of a human without emotion.

As the children formed their lines, Cassie paid careful attention to him today. She knew where Ethan fit in all of this, but not Draven.

His dark eyes narrowed as he surveyed the room. Yellow tie, black jacket, and dress slacks ... Cassie had taken to noting every detail she could. Still hoping one day she would have someone to share them with.

"It's the business *we* run now, Ethan." Draven's voice was calm, his demeanor aloof.

Cassie could easily see the man did not care what Ethan thought.

"We are taking a new turn," Draven explained further. "There is more money in this market, and they are easier to obtain."

"I give a job to a woman willing to work. I don't drug them; I don't abuse them. I give them a safe place to work. That's my business."

Draven laughed and waved him off. "That is not nearly as profitable. But I see that you have acclimated nicely to the challenge. Using storage units was genius. And you have to admit the supply chain is plentiful. I believe you will continue to grow—with my help, of course."

Ethan glanced around the room and cringed at the sight. When three patrons entered behind him, he did not hide his disdain. He kept his distance as though they were diseased. The overhead lights buzzed softly, and the children made no sound.

"I told you, Draven, he would be malleable," said the woman who had just arrived. "With my contacts, we can find merchandise in order to fit anyone's preference. Ethan provides the place to store them. It's a fantastic partnership!" the woman declared; her voice gravelly—no doubt the result of decades of smoking.

She had been there before. Many times. Discreetly, Cassie took Anna's hand and felt the child begin to tremble.

"Harriet." Ethan's tone was low and dangerous.

"You have yet to deliver on your promise, Harriet." Draven's tone was cutting. Cassie saw the woman's shocked reaction at the reprimand. Draven walked out without another word.

The woman turned her attention to the line-up of children, dismissing him with a wave only after the door closed behind him. "We'll talk more later, Ethan," she promised.

Ethan turned his attention to his property. Cassie tried to imagine what he saw when he looked at them. Who knew? Maybe he had a sliver of humanity buried deep in his soul. She could only hope. It would be that last sliver that she could appeal to.

When the time was right, and the Lord opened the door.

The way of this dark world had made itself plain in a short time. Sometimes the clients came here, made their selection, and would travel to another location. Like Cassie's first visit with "Daddy." A rented room of obscurity where a bogeyman could steal innocence. The dank, musty room of a seedy motel, the odor of past couples hanging in the air. Others would rent the penthouse. They had money and power and a position to protect. They hid deep in the shadows of night yet walked freely in the light of day. The clientele ranged from street scum to politicians. This debauchery knew no class restrictions.

Today, customers were hungrily eyeing their options as their options stole furtive glances in their direction. The first client, a good-looking man in his thirties, wore a three-piece suit. At least he seemed clean. He stood close enough for Cassie to catch his earthy cologne. While his smile made her skin crawl, he didn't strike her as violent. But between this room and the next, a monster could easily take his place.

Drawing closer to Cassie, a girl named Shayna quivered as she took her hand. Lily was standing in front of Cassie and pressing her tiny frame into her, probably hoping to blend in—or better yet, disappear.

Every time the clients would come in, Cassie fought the bile in her throat. Not from fear, though. From rage. She had mastered the plastic come-hither smile and softened her eyes in an attempt to lure the fiends away from the younger kids. Sadly, most of them didn't even want her—she was too old. They wanted Anna or Lily. Some asked for Tommy. It took every ounce of self-control for Cassie not to attack. She often envisioned herself taking them all down the same way she had Sarah and her friends. In that long-ago, faraway life she once lived. But she was smart and steady. She knew it was best to bide her time and make a plan.

The trouble was, she had no idea where they were, so how could there be a plan? And how could she get the kids out with her? These little ones had become her priority. Maybe it gave her purpose, but she endeavored to protect them. It seemed with every passing day that she was driven more to prayer. Truly it was her last resort. She desperately hoped that God was still in the business of mountain moving.

The next man, maybe in his fifties but in denial about it, wore an untucked shirt under a relaxed white blazer and jeans. Cassie remembered that her dad held the opinion that men with money and little character wore tassels on their loafers. This guy wore tassels. And he chose Tommy and Rose.

The third was the woman Ethan had referred to as Harriet. Apparently, life had not been kind to her. Heavyset, wrinkles around the lips and yellow-tinged skin—she was probably only in her forties, looking well into her sixties. She had on a long flowing dress with a bright print, seemingly unaware of how the material added inches to her broad figure. Leather sandals covered her fat feet. Her chubby toes with gnarly nails hung off the ends of the shoes.

She held herself with a casual ugliness as she surveyed the options in front of her. Landing her vulture eyes on her favorite selection, she moved toward the line of children. "You could at least clean them up for the amount of money we pay you, Ethan," she said without taking her eyes off her choice. "They look pitiful. You really should take better care of your merchandise." She snarled, obviously unafraid to voice her opinion. "I suppose you will, now that Draven is involved in your affairs." She sounded smug.

Ethan bristled.

"Oh," she chided him. "You should be thrilled that I pointed him in your direction, Ethan." She spoke with such superiority.

Cassie watched as Ethan balled his hands into fists at his sides.

"Now that we are working together, I expect to have some say in what matters. Namely, keeping our business in such disarray. I mean really, I am now *personally* invested here." Harriet smiled at Ethan's reaction.

His eyebrows were drawn tightly together; his mouth was a thin line. "Harriet." His tone dripped with venom and fury. "You have no impact on my business aside from being a paying customer. Make your selection."

She ran her thick fingers through Anna's brown curls. "Blue eyes."

A soft whisper meant for Anna, but Cassie was close enough to hear too. Anna lowered her head in submission and walked out with her. Cassie's hand curled into a fist, and she forced herself to relax. She repeated the rules in her mind: *Look good. Obey. Don't talk to anyone.* Only pleasant behavior was allowed in front of the clients.

As Harriet walked to the door, Anna in tow, she paused at Ethan's side and looked up at him. "Another thing, Ethan." She spoke with an air of authority. "I want the coven's emblem on every one of your crates."

Shrugging as if to say he would consider it, he did not deign to look at her. The muscle in his jaw clenched.

She continued, "I'm sure Draven will see the wisdom in this idea. It will bring honor to the master. We will mark our business for his glory."

She smirked as she walked out of the rectangle room.

While the other clients took their time making their selections, Cassie prayed—soft and fervently.

My God, El Roi—the God who sees— Discouraged and afraid, she pleaded in desperate prayer. *Please. Protect them, Jesus. Send us help! Somehow ...*

Even as the words played in her mind, hope faded like dandelion fuzz on the wind. She had lived years since coming here, such a short time ago. Days filled with horror resulted in faith that dwindled to nothing. *If He is going to move on our behalf, it will not be through my prayers.*

But she thought she saw a light flash in the shadows. She swore she felt demons tremble.

Twelve

Melody settled into her favorite chair as she tapped the green icon on her phone.

"Hello, Melody?" Mae Murphy's bold Southern drawl brought a smile to Melody's face even as she quickly turned down the volume on her phone. "It's Mae."

"Hi, Mae." Melody eased the phone back to a comfortable position. "How are you?"

"Oh, I'm good, dear. I wanted to touch base. See how you and the family are doing." Mae practically sang as she spoke.

Makes sense. Melody thought. *She's led the choir for nearly fifteen years.*

"Oh, we're all good! How is Frank?" Melody picked up her journal and began absently flipping through the pages.

"As cantankerous as ever. That man." Mae snorted with derision.

Melody knew she was about to take a deep dive, so she placed the journal on the side table, connected to her AirPods, and grabbed the leash. She could multitask while Mae vented. Cooper was already at the door.

"He doesn't want me to take this new job. I am excited about it, Melody. But he says I don't need to work, and he doesn't want his sanctuary to be affected. As if I would slack on my home duties. But I'm bored, and I want something to do. It's just part-time. I think I can handle it," she ended with a heavy sigh.

Melody assessed the dark clouds brewing to the west. She felt confident she could take Cooper around the block before the rains came. She and Mae had been friends for more than twenty years. Recognizing the way that Mae asked for advice, Melody prepared a response as she threw on a light jacket and headed out the door.

"Well, friend, I think he has a point." She heard Mae huff. "But so do you. It's not a bad thing to want more from your life. But why do you want to do it?"

"I don't know. I feel restless. Like FOMO or something," Mae lamented.

Melody held back her laughter. "Do you know what FOMO means, Mae?" Cooper raced as far as the leash would allow him.

"Well, of course, I do, Melody! I may be pushing seventy, but I'm still with it, girl." Mae chuckled at herself. "But I do have a fear of missing out. And I feel like I still have a lot of *doing* left in me. I certainly don't feel like I'm *done!*"

"Okay, I understand that. Let's consider all that you are doing now." Melody began to rattle off all of Mae's commitments … at least the ones she knew about. "You lead the choir every week."

"I can do that with my eyes closed, Melody."

"You teach Sunday school to first graders."

"You know you teach the same concepts every year. It's just the kids that change."

"And lead a weekly Bible study in your home."

"As a leader, you just need to study and then let the ladies do the talking. I have plenty of time to study."

"You organize the convalescent home visits."

"That's just a good investment in my future, dear."

"You have your house, your husband." Melody heard Mae scoff. "Your kids."

"They don't need me anymore." Mae's voice held a hint of a pout.

"Your grandkids."

"They're schooling during the day, and the job offers flexibility. I can even work remotely if I need to, the ad says."

"Well, it appears you've thought this through." Melody pulled Cooper away from a knocked-down garbage can. Small drops began to sprinkle from the clouds. *Shoot, that came quick. I thought I'd have more time. A short walk today, Cooper Boy.* "What did Frank say, exactly?"

"That I can take it if I feel *compelled*." She groaned. "I've been with this man for nearly fifty years, and I still don't know if that is a yes or a no!"

"Oh, Mae, Frank would never hold you back. He's just trying to get you to keep balance. You know you say yes to every request that bounces across your path. You haven't wanted to work outside the home for twenty years. Why the push now?"

"I don't know." Mae hesitated. "I did some research into this company, Human Potential, and I got a nudge. You know, Melody—a Holy Spirit nudge."

Now Melody's smile broadened. "Well, why didn't you start with that? Tell me about the company." Not only did that mean that God was leading something; it also meant Mae had gone into detective mode. Her research could give Agatha Christie a run for her money.

"It's been around for almost twelve years. Same owner, and they are heavily involved in charity and community support. I just love that. I would be the administrative assistant to the owner, Ethan Walker. He's somewhere in his thirties, real sharp-looking from what I could find on the internet. Although there was surprisingly little to find. There is something there, Melody, and I'd like to find out what it is. I haven't felt a nudge like this since the mission fields of Kenya."

"Go for it, then. If Frank is okay, then apply. If the door opens, great. If it closes, great! Either way, you know God is in it."

"Well, that sounds like some solid wisdom," Mae trilled.

Melody chuckled. "Of course, it is, Mae. You're the one who taught me!"

They laughed together.

Melody recalled something she wanted to ask Mae. "Oh, Mae, one more thing."

"Sure, what is it?"

"I reconnected with a friend from the church. Do you remember Beth Everett?"

"Sure do. I have Esther in my class right now. It was such a tragic thing they went through last year with the baby," Mae noted sorrowfully.

"Yes, she's in the thick of life right now. Homeschooling both the girls, new house. Her husband is a detective—you know that has to be a stressful job. Anyway, I wanted to start a Bible study and thought you may be interested. Of course, that was before the new job—"

"Oh, nonsense! I'd love to. Just send me the details, and I'll pencil you in!"

"Great. See you this week, then. Good luck with the job."

"Thanks, dear. See you soon."

Melody chuckled again as she hit the red button to end the call. *Mae Murphy said FOMO.* She laughed harder, racing Cooper back to the house as the first crack of thunder split the sky.

Thirteen

Cassie woke with a start. The hand over her mouth was only one reason. The hand under her shirt was the other. She fought to move but James was on top of her. Her screams were muffled behind his immovable hand. In his frenzy, he was whispering his love for her.

Bile burned the back of her throat. She understood that, having been raised in this world, he would have no knowledge of what love truly was. How could he? But at this moment, she truly did not care.

He had his way, despite the contents of her stomach lying on the floor beside her. In the aftermath, he tried to hold her. She was limp in his arms, filled with despair and hopelessness.

Will this be my life now? A man's pawn to be used and tossed away?

The tears fell down the arm that cradled her head as she wept for the loss of all she had once known and the fear that her future was as dark as the room where she was kept.

"I love you, Cassie," he whispered in his ecstasy.

She sobbed.

Finally he left, but not before placing a repulsive morning-breath kiss on her, which she didn't move in time to block. She loathed him more now than ever before and was dangerously close to making a mistake that would end her chances of survival. But something reined her in.

That's right, she reminded herself. She reached out and ran a finger softly down Lily's face as she slept. Swiping away the tears, she hardened her resolve. *The others. I have to think of the others. This can't all be happening for no reason. I have to keep hoping. I have to fan this failing flame of faith. My survival depends on it.*

In the days following James's visit, Cassie tended to several new arrivals. Among them were Maria, who had crossed over the Mexican border, forced here at the hands of drug-running coyotes when her stepbrother sold her into slavery. Danny was from Cleveland, and ten-year-old Gaelle had been stolen from Haiti. Gaelle remembered being forced into a shipping container along with about twenty other women, girls, and boys. It was a large, steel rectangle, much like what they were in now. It must have been a long, lonely journey for her. Cassie's heart ached.

Constantly trying her best to remember the details she had discovered since her arrival, Cassie repeated the tidbits of information. The street names, the license plate, and the movie theater. Worry filled her at the thought of forgetting anything. Not that she had any idea what she would do with the information, but still. Running through the details in her mind helped her remain calm. It was as if they were somehow a lifeline back to her past—and her sanity.

The temperature had fallen, and they found it harder to stay warm in their steel cage. Obviously, they weren't in Florida anymore. So many details from the night of her abduction had been obliterated by whatever they'd used to knock her out. She remembered seeing Ethan on the street that night, and then … nothing. Did the mongrels just throw her duffel bag away?

The next thing she remembered, she woke up in a dirty van, and the rest of the nightmare she refused to relive. But now that she had some details, embers of hope seemed to glow in her heart. Again, she realized she was rubbing the finger absent from the ring. It was becoming a habit whenever she lost herself in thought.

Shouting from the far end of the rectangle drew Cassie from her reverie. Fear made smart people do stupid things. Not that this new arrival, who had

Fields of Gomorrah

come in last night, was stupid—she might have been a genius. But in this place, she got stupid. With broken glasses and an ugly snarl, she seemed possessed by a rabid pit bull. She was a big girl with thin wavy hair that had turned greasy in the days since her last shower.

Cassie observed her for the first couple of hours. They had brought her in during the night. She was violent and cursed like a seasoned trucker, and it took the guards some time to settle her down. Somehow, she had managed to bring in a plastic fork. It would have been easy enough in her cargo pants or black combat boots. The guards were quick and abusive more than thorough.

Her outfit struck a chill in Cassie. It had been July when she herself was taken. If this girl was in boots and flannel, then the chill of fall must have settled in. *My birthday is October first. Have I missed it?* The thoughts came unbidden. Unfortunately, the movie was already playing.

Mentally, she wandered back to that ill-fated day, replaying it as she often had since her arrival. Wishing with all she had to be able to go back and change everything, make new choices, and free herself from this prison.

She traveled back in her memory, resting in her grandmother's rocking chair after a huge fight with her mom, walking around her room—her sanctuary. Together, she and her mother had sorted out every detail last summer. The walls were painted a soft gray—it was trendy, but she loved it. Fuzzy pillows in cream and dusty blue lined the bed with a fabric headboard. A handmade quilt from her grandmother was folded at the foot of the bed. A desk sat in front of the window, and her Bible was open to Ephesians 6. She could almost feel the cool breeze as she imagined sitting at her desk to study.

The low, solid wood dresser with six drawers boasted a large mirror. Pictures shoved into the sides of its frame smiled back at her. Cassie and her mom in a goofy selfie photo. A homecoming picture with Daddy was just under that. And of course, with BFF, Kendra, ear-to-ear teenage smiles. On top of the dresser, neatly arranged treasures—from favorite snapshots and movie tickets to makeup, perfume, and jewelry from her dad. Her room had been a haven and a reflection of the girl she knew she never would be again.

Resigned to the fact that she would never be able to go back to the moment she left, Cassie prayed she would be able to hug her mom at least one more time. To feel the arms of her father strong around her shoulders. She forced all the memories from her mind, her mother's face being the last image to fade as the sounds came back into focus, and with them the pitiful girl in the rectangle room. She sighed, realizing she was the pitiful girl.

Cassie ventured over to the new girl, not sure what to expect, and keeping a wary eye on her. A thin strand of wayward hair floated in front of her face as she held a white plastic fork in her hand, mumbling about a bizarre plan in incoherent babble.

"Hey." Cassie's regular greeting. "What's your name?"

"Why do you do this?" Missy called from across the room.

"It's hard enough, Missy. To feel alone makes it even worse."

"You really shouldn't make connections, Cassie," Missy advised.

Cassie knew she was right but pressed forward anyway. Cassie squatted down to be level with the girl's face. Missy shook her head and rolled over onto her side.

"Trudy." The girl offered in a growl. "And she's right. I don't need to get to know you. I won't be here long. I'm getting out of here. I already have a plan."

Cassie recognized the desperation in her voice. Same as Jazmin.

"Where are you from, Trudy?" Cassie asked. She tried to keep a mental list of all the kids and their locations. Despite her weak faith, she still hoped to be rescued. Someday.

"Minnesota" was Trudy's one-word reply; still, she did not turn to look at Cassie.

She was plump and soft, and Cassie didn't see a physique that matched a fighter. She tried to reason with her: "Listen, fear and desperation, they can influence us to do some really risky things."

"I am not scared." Trudy proudly held up the fork in her hand. "I've got a plan, and if you want to join me, I can get us both out of here." Her eyes were wide and rapidly shifted back and forth.

Cassie tried to get through the panic. "I don't think you have processed everything you are up against here."

"I won't have your negativity. Stop talking." She was blunt and rude and threw up a hand of dismissal in Cassie's face.

Cassie knew there was no dealing with such an obstinate person. She asked her to reconsider and returned to her spot. She sat down and prayed, *Lord, that could have been me. I am a hothead too. Stubborn and prideful. Somehow, I have survived this long. However long it has been … But I feel You here with me, in this dark prison. I know You'll avenge me, free me … heal me. I know You will fight for me—I need only be still. I know there is not a thing I can do but wait upon You, Lord. But Your Word tells me, I will mount up with wings like an eagle. I pray that day is very soon.*

Taking Lily's hand in hers and tenderly brushing back some hair from Anna's face, Cassie instructed them, "When the guards come, don't look up. Keep your head down. You don't need to see what is coming."

Her wisdom rang true. When the door opened, Trudy rushed the guard. She had the power behind her and was apparently used to using it. However, being the size of a Mack truck was in Melvin's favor, not to mention the machine gun that hung from his shoulder. Or the knife at his waist that could fillet her face. Fear made you do stupid really well. One solid blow to her head and she landed, writhing in pain, on the cold floor, clutching her bloody brow.

She wailed and moaned until the guard's boot crashed down on her face, knocking her unconscious.

As the guards opened the door to remove the girl, James ambled in. He carried a pot of oatmeal, the standard fare. He noticed the child on the floor only enough to shuffle around her. He did not seem to be impacted by anything. Except for Cassie. A crooked smile broke across his face when he spotted her. She cringed. The memory of what he had done to her weakened her.

For some reason she could not quite figure out, this man had become infatuated with her. He served her first. He always held some back to see if she wanted more. He brought her trinkets and wrote her notes. He had not touched her since that dreadful day.

The man disgusted her, and she really did not know what to make of his attention or how to handle it. Recently, she decided to use it to her advantage. Cautious to answer his questions, to allow him any insight that he could use against her, she charmed him.

"I brought you something, Cassie." He smiled shyly. "I have a pen for you. I'll get you some paper. I remember you said you like to draw."

Anna peered at the gift from behind Cassie. The last thing Cassie wanted to do was touch the pen but thought how good it would be to write down all those facts she had been collecting.

Cassie heard Missy laugh. She ignored it, but James did not.

"Hey, girl. Don't you laugh at Cassie," he yelled, pouting. Cassie wondered at how he would stand up for her, but not himself.

Cassie softly turned his face away from Missy. "It's okay, James. She is allowed to laugh." Hoping she might be able to plant some seeds in his mind that could lead him to do the right thing, she continued. "We should all be free, right, James?" She looked at him, making her eyes wide and trusting, taking the pen from him.

He shrugged. "Well, I suppose it's okay to laugh."

Cassie sighed and reminded herself you need soil for seeds, and he seemed to be an empty, void wasteland.

That night, Cassie dreamed of a field. Vast acreage full of golden wheat, up to her waist. As she walked through, she let the stalks run against her palms. A soft breeze brushed her skin. She saw a dark cloud on the horizon as the winds increased from balmy to blasting. The wind brought clouds of locusts, and she ducked and covered as they descended upon the rows of plants. In moments, the field was laid bare. She was now in a barren field. Bent and broken stalks, empty of their bounty, littered the space that had been rich and full.

She moved toward a sound—a crying baby. There in the center of the field lay a child wrapped in a blue blanket. Suddenly, the ground, hard and dry, began to crack around her. She lunged for the child and scooped him up, screaming as the earth gave way and they tumbled into a dark, bottomless pit. She looked up and saw her parents on the edge of the abyss. Two women she didn't know were there too. Shadows blocked their faces from sight.

She awoke in a sweat as panic gripped her and the darkness smothered her. She slowed her breathing, which eased her racing heart. *It hurts to see their faces, even in a dream, Lord. I so desperately want to be with them. Please restore us. Bring me home.*

Fourteen

Beth and Melody gathered at the table in Melody's kitchen. The girls would be at a playdate for three hours. Beth had been looking forward to this time of Bible study since setting it up last week. They had agreed to read the first chapter of Deuteronomy and talk through what God showed them.

A knock sounded at the door, and a voice trilled down the hall into the kitchen. "Melody, I'm here. I'm sorry I'm late, dear." Melody and Beth exchanged happy smiles. Mae jostled to the table, balancing her purse, Bible, and canvas tote, along with a decadent-looking chocolate cake.

"Mae! You shouldn't have." Melody clapped before taking the tempting cake and setting it on the counter.

"You won't say that after the first bite." Mae chuckled as she settled at the table, spreading out her journal, Bible, and a selection of pens and highlighters. With a wink at Beth, she confessed, "I have a thing for pens!"

Beth offered her hand. "Mrs. Murphy, it's so nice to finally meet you!"

"It's Mae, please." She took Beth's hand and shook it vigorously. Her grandmotherly frame filled the kitchen chair as her welcoming heart filled the kitchen.

The ladies made small talk about motherhood, retirement, and new beginnings before holding hands and bowing their heads as Melody led the prayer.

"Dear Jesus, please bless this time of study so that we can learn the things You have for us. Reveal Yourself through Your Word, and show us amazing things! In Jesus's name, amen!"

Beth pulled the notebook and Bible out of her brown leather satchel. She treasured journals the way Mae did pens and seemed to have one for every need. Journaling was a great tool for her to capture her thoughts, share her hopes, and be mindful of her blessings. Today's journal was specific to the Bible study with her new friends.

"How is Frank, Mae?" Melody flipped through her Bible and laid it on the table.

"As ornery as ever."

"Kids?"

"Busy with life and no time for their old mother."

"Grandkids?"

Mae's smile was broad, and she talked for several minutes about each of the six grandkids.

"And how is Scott?" Mae asked Melody.

"Oh, as ornery as ever." They both enjoyed a laugh.

Looking at the two ladies, Beth asked, "How long have you two known each other?" Mae and Melody exchanged glances. Beth laughed. "Do you remember?"

"Mae and I worked together at the doctor's office, so we've known about each other for a while. But our friendship really blossomed after I started going to church with her." Melody's voice was a song as she shared the memories. "I was still single then, to give you some timeline. Scott was in the picture, but we were just friends. I thought I needed more time to 'be independent.'" It was Melody's turn to laugh now.

Mae joined in. "I knew those two were meant to be. He was like a lost puppy looking for home, and he found it when they were together. He just adored her. Still does." She beamed. "I had quite the hand at matchmaking when I was younger!"

"Yes, and you still do." Melody pointed a finger in her direction. "Grace told me all about your conversation the other night." The twinkle in Melody's eye belied her accusation.

87

Mae burst out in a robust laugh, smacking the table and wheezing. "I know, I know. Guilty as charged. But, Melody, I haven't lost my touch yet!"

They continued their conversation for a few more moments until eventually Melody segued into the reason for their meeting.

"Well, let's get started ... I never realized Deuteronomy had so much to offer. I'll be honest—" Melody began, clicking her blue ballpoint pen. "I thought it would be dry. But did you see in chapter 1, around verse 19, how the Israelites had the opportunity to walk right into the Promised Land, but they decided not to?"

"Right," Beth agreed, nodding her head and flipping to a page in her book. "Yes! I saw that too. Their disobedience to God's instruction cost them their promise. Oh, I wonder what promises I have been disobedient to."

For a moment, Beth considered the loss of her son. Surely, that had not been an issue of obedience. Emotion threatened to overwhelm her, and she pushed down the pain. While she did not know why her son had to die, she was not ready to process that in front of her friends quite yet.

Beth shook her head slightly but caught the careful tender eye of Mae on her. She smiled weakly and was grateful when Melody continued.

"Well, I think we know when we are in disobedience, right?" Melody proposed. After a pause, she continued, "Like, to be transparent, when I disobey God there are usually some other factors at play; mostly I am not trusting Him, or I doubt His promises ... something else preempts the disobedience."

Her words eased the anxiety in Beth's heart.

"Obedience is the first step." Mae shared her wisdom freely. "Without it, we silence God's Spirit and with it, we open the doors. It is a linchpin in the relationship between us and our Savior."

"That's true. I can really struggle with pride. Thinking I know what's best and God should just catch up. And if He doesn't, then I press on, not usually in the way I should go." Beth chewed on the tip of her pen as she often did when processing ideas. "I guess if we can identify the issue that triggers us, we can turn it over to God—you know, release it before it leads

Fields of Gomorrah

to disobedience." Beth looked to her friend for reassurance. She was still shy in sharing her thoughts with other people.

Melody gazed back at her. "What a valuable thought, Beth. That is excellent. I'm going to write that down and start asking God to show me what my triggers are. And I'll start watching for them." She paused in her writing. "I guess it is a team effort of sorts. When I'm obedient, I can hear His voice. When I start to stray, I have a decision to make: listen to God calling me out, or shut Him down and do my own thing."

Mae tapped Beth's notebook. "I see you also like to journal. That is a very good tool to use to identify your strengths and struggles."

"Well, I really want to hear Him." Beth sighed. "I don't want to miss what He has in store for me."

"But what if, I mean ... I guess I wrestle with the possibility that God's plan, even though it is good, could still be difficult. How open am I to that?"

Beth gave Melody credit. She was certainly honest.

"I guess it's equally possible that the trial will come anyway. How do we manage through it makes the difference?" Beth's brows furrowed. "Like when we found out we couldn't have any more children—and then we lost William." Her voice cracked. She cleared her throat and rolled her head to the side. She couldn't stop the moisture in her eyes.

Melody reached over and took her hand.

"When we lost our baby, if it wasn't for God's peace and presence, I don't think I would have survived. Knowing we couldn't have another—"

"I'm so sorry, Beth. Thank you for sharing that." Mae comforted her, placing her hand softly on Beth's arm. "I know it is not easy to speak of loss and pain. And I agree with you. When I lost my little Trinity, it was only God that saw me through the pain."

Both Melody and Beth looked at Mae in surprise.

"I had no idea you lost a child," Melody exclaimed. "I thought Thomas and Abigail ..."

Mae continued, "Yes. At two years old. A terrible accident. We adopted Thomas nearly a year after, and Abigail followed close behind. But Beth is correct—it rains on the just and the unjust alike, and the trials will likely come regardless of our posture toward God, just as the opportunity to enter Canaan came to the Israelites. They had the choice to obey and walk with God or disobey and feel His presence removed. So, rain or shine, I think I'd rather be in His presence." Mae rummaged through her purse and handed Beth a tissue, pulling one out for herself as well. "He is our shelter in the storm." She dabbed at the moisture in her eyes.

Melody pushed her chair back from the table. "How about some of that cake?" she asked with a bright smile.

Beth appreciated the interruption. And that cake really did look delicious.

Fifteen

At his desk in his den, Billy scrolled through images on his computer, searching for any connection to the snake in a circle. He usually had the large window open to allow the fall breeze to flow through, but today he had drawn the blinds to reduce the glare on his computer screen. The etchings on the slide at the playground had reached from the center top of the structure to where it met the metal frame that held it. A half circle filled with the repeated drawing. He rubbed his chin, lost in thought as he absently adjusted his reading glasses. *And Dixon didn't mention it at all.*

The file of Lily Chamberlain lay open on his desk, the contents spread out as he had rummaged through it looking for any clues, any connections. He'd found none.

He looked up as Beth quietly slipped into the room. She only came in to straighten up his den when she had something on her mind. She was dusting around the bookshelf, edging closer to him. He felt her eyes on him. He pulled off his glasses, set them to the side of his keyboard, and swiveled around to speak with her.

"Hello, dear." He chuckled. "Is there something you wanted to talk about?"

She returned the smile and sank into the easy chair by the bookshelf.

"How are you? How is your case?" She was stalling.

"It's not good." He rubbed his temple and stretched his neck. "It's rough, babe. Knowing how she was taken. You know I can't share much, but for the sake of our girls—you should know there are kids being used to lure the victims away. Please be careful when you're out, Beth. You really cannot trust anyone. And don't go to the parks across town; stay close to home."

"I know. I talk with Melody about that all the time. Speaking of Melody, remember the Bible study I started with her?" She fidgeted with the feather duster in her hand.

"Yes, her husband is Scott, right?"

"Mmm, yeah." She seemed to be somewhere else. Billy angled his chair a little toward his desk, hoping she would take the hint. "We bumped into each other at the grocery store. Literally." She smiled.

"Esther?" he asked, and they both laughed.

She leaned forward with her elbows on her knees, flipping the feather duster in her hand. "Yes, it was! But it was good. She has a lot of information on homeschooling, and we started a Bible study."

"Yeah, you mentioned that. Deuteronomy, right?" He shifted in his chair, eager to get back to his search.

"I …" She hesitated. "I spoke about William."

He sat silent for a long moment.

"I'm sorry," she stammered, starting to get up from the chair and shaking her head. "I know you don't like—"

"That's great, Beth." He spoke softly, his tone empty of emotion. The rift was still fresh in his heart. "You needed some friends to talk with … I know I haven't—" He struggled, broke off, and redirected. "I'm so glad." He turned back to his work, watching her in the reflection of his sleeping computer screen.

She moved toward the door. She paused with one hand on the doorknob. "Okay, well. I guess I just wanted you to know." He turned to see her wiping her eyes as she left the room. Words wouldn't come to his mind.

He returned to his work, putting the conversation out of his mind and his child back in the grave. He had not been emotionally available since the incident. He couldn't be. He buried himself back into his research. Focus on children that he could save.

Images flashed across the screen. Snakes inside pentagrams. Pentagrams surrounded by snakes. Necklaces. Earrings. Jpeg images. Posters. Satan. All disturbing. None of what he was looking for. He changed the search from "pentagrams and serpents" to "pentagram serpent logo."

Pushing back from the desk, he ran his hands through his hair in frustration. Thoughts of his baby swirled around with the face of Lily in his mind. He groaned deep within.

Lord, show me what I'm missing.

After a few moments with no resulting shock of lightning or his laptop scrolling on its own to a specific logo, Billy closed the browser and opened his email. Several messages had come through since he left work, and he sorted through them to see if anything was important. One email was sent to his attention from his partner, Dixon.

> Hey, Billy,
> I'm sorry I didn't make it to the office today. Fill me in on
> the case today. I will be out again tomorrow.

Dixon did not sign off on the quick note. Billy wondered briefly what his partner was up to. Obviously, he wasn't sick. Not on vacation. But not being transparent, either.

He opened the search engine one last time. He typed in a new search option and searched by image, "businesses with serpent logos." Halfway down the third page, he paused.

The Wisdom Foundation.

A tiny image followed the tagline—"helping humanity"—a subtle logo that could be interpreted as the serpent devouring itself. A broken circle with a backward arrow on one end, with a point locking into the opening of the first arrow, centered inside a star.

Billy clicked on the image, which brought him to the company website. He moved the mouse to the menu at the bottom of the page and selected "About."

The next page flashed up with headshots of several employees and their titles. Billy stopped short when he saw the first name on the board of directors—Draven Wolfe.

Draven Wolfe. The business magnate seemed to have his hand in every level of society. If rumors held truth, this man funded several nefarious groups. Some of which were on the FBI's terrorist watch list.

Of course, it was just a supposition with no proof. It might be nothing, he thought. *It may be everything.*

He continued to go through the website, one menu at a time. He learned very little. What they did was vague. "Helping humanity center their conscience." *Whatever that means.*

He found some programs. Detox Your Spirit: A Twelve-Day Program to Free Your Inner Self; Better You: Revealing the Inner Channels of Your Being to Further Your Success.

And some articles: "Free of Addiction: Lead Your Mind to a Healthy Body." "Chanting in the Twenty-First Century: Returning to the Past to Restore Your Future." "Find Your Mantra: Identifying the Spirit Guide Within."

Billy took furious notes, printed pages of information, and added them to the file. He found the logo, blew it up onto a full-size sheet of paper, and printed it out. He held it up to the slide images. It was a rough comparison, but it was the first connection he had found.

He piled it all together, shoving pages into the file. It was late now, nearly one in the morning. He closed the laptop and then laid the file in the bottom drawer of his desk. Leaning back in his chair, he rubbed his eyes and stretched his body.

He stood, then slipped out of the den and crept down the hall. Peeking in on the girls, he smiled and made his way to his bedroom. Beth lay sleeping on the bed, curled on her side. He brushed her face with a soft kiss, regretting dismissing her earlier that night. After dressing in his pajamas, he climbed into the bed and snuggled close to his wife.

Even in her sleep, she responded to his touch and mumbled a soft "Love you" before drifting back to dreamland.

Fields of Gomorrah

Billy smiled as he held her, so thankful for her. He drifted off to sleep.

During the night, he battled demons in his dreams, fighting for a blond-haired little girl and a baby wrapped in a blue blanket.

Sixteen

Melody filled three machines with the clothes from her family of five for the week. *I'll be doing laundry until they're all married,* she thought.

Two baskets sat in the back of her SUV—towels, and sheets that were washed, dried, and folded. The sweet scent of detergent filled the air. The melodic squeaking of the machines and thumping of the dryers filled the room with their pleasant, rhythmic sound.

She wished she could say the same about the company. It was a well-to-do neighborhood, but the laundromat didn't seem to know that. Two ladies lingered in the back of the room having a loud conversation. Passionate, but not quite yelling; lots of cackling. The young man who hovered by the door tensely watched the street from the large window. His oversized shirt did little to conceal the fact that his pants were almost falling to his knees. He seemed anxious. But didn't hide the lingering gaze as he turned to watch Melody loading the washing machine.

She hurried with the last load, eager to leave the machines to do their thing. She would let these run for the next forty-five minutes while she read her Bible and spent some time in prayer—away from the laundromat.

The broken washer at home served to be a blessing in disguise. She laughed out loud, while filling the tub with blue jeans, thinking of the conversation she'd had with her husband.

"Are you sure you don't want a new washer?" He had sounded so confused. "Where is my reasonable, level-headed woman?"

They had been standing in the kitchen. He buttered the toast while she fried some eggs.

"No, I really don't." She flipped an egg and let out a small curse when the yolk broke. "I like doing this once a week and being done! And we don't need to spend the money right now, babe. I'm really okay with this. When I'm not, I'll let you know." She gave him a sassy smile.

He smiled in return, set his toast down, and walked over to her. "Well, I have no doubts that you'll let me know." He drew her to him and kissed her softly.

She responded as her arms curled behind his head, running her fingers through his salt-and-pepper hair. His hands hung low and loose around her waist.

"I'll take the broken egg." He nodded in the direction of the pan as if taking a bullet.

She laughed. "We can give that one to Alex. He won't even notice!"

As if on cue, their son wandered into the kitchen in his pajama bottoms and no shirt. They caught the look on his face when he saw them, and he turned around and walked back out of the kitchen. Their laughter filled the kitchen.

That was where she found herself today. She laughed softly in the open room with the walls lined with washers and dryers. Now, once a week, she made her way to the laundromat to crank out a chore most women dreaded. She sorted all the clothes at home, loaded up her SUV, and lugged five baskets into machines. She got all the family's laundry done in one day—washed and dried, anyway. Putting it away would forever be a challenge. It was a sacrifice she was willing to make until their finances were in a better place.

With the last two loads in the washing machines, and moving one into the dryer, she worked quickly, eager and ready to return to her truck.

Melody began to pray, comfortably seated behind the steering wheel. She had parked at the far end of the lot. A sense of urgency and a thrill to connect with her Savior refreshed her soul and ignited her heart. The words fell from her lips. A mysterious connection that made sense outside the human experience. As the Holy Spirit led, the words came from her soul directly to God's throne. This wondrous gift that she had only just begun using connected her to a world beyond what she could touch and see.

Melody was thoughtful as she prayed, turning her heart to listen to what the Lord had to say. Often, a word or two would come to her mind. As the words came now, she jotted them down and tucked the notebook back into her bag and returned to the laundromat.

She finished the laundry, moving the last two loads from washer to dryer and folding what she had just pulled out. The clothes were warm against her skin as she folded them, thinking of her prayer. The last word rolled around in her mind, and she found herself quite excited to look up the meaning and call her friend.

When Melody settled back into the driver's seat, she put on some worship music and opened her notebook. She had just about an hour before the last of the laundry was dry.

She looked at the short list of words she had been given over the past several weeks. With her, near, together.

Twice, she had received "restriction, limitation, demarcation."

Then, "Take back, respond, reply, answer." She realized she had received that one twice as well.

She added today's word to the record and trembled in a mix of nerves and excitement.

"Walking. March."

Seventeen

Beth woke with her heart racing. She struggled to move, as the sleep paralysis held her in place. The sheet stuck to the perspiration on her skin. She lay in confusion, mixing what she had just been dreaming with her waking reality. She counted to ten, and slowly the hold of the dream faded, and she was able to move again. She felt the bed next to her ... empty. Billy had the night shift. Her mind paused as she lay back on her pillow. The feeling of urgency did not fade. She felt compelled to go check on her two daughters.

She padded down the hall and softly opened the door to the girls' room. Two twin beds lined the far wall, and the children lay peacefully sleeping in them. Beth released the breath she had not realized she was holding. Esther was lying sideways in the bed, and Maggie had kicked off all her blankets. Beth crossed the room and tucked the blankets around Maggie. Two small steps and she was at Esther's bed. She straightened her out and placed a kiss on the child's forehead. They were safe.

Someone's daughter was not.

As she returned to her room, her mind was tearing into the dream. It must have been real—a vision. It was too vivid. She remembered every detail. The fear, the urgency in the girl who wore first a dirty negligee and then somehow a pleasant hunter-green dress. And the hypnotized crowd of worshippers, faces the child had frantically searched in the hopes of finding anyone that would help her.

The snake of a man standing at the altar ... what did he say? Why could she remember so much of the vision, but not the words he spoke? She was instantly in prayer.

To protect you from his lies. The thought popped into her mind as if in response to her question.

Ah, yes. That makes sense.

She sat down at her desk, flipping on the Tiffany lamp she had inherited from her mother. She called it her prayer light. It was dim and warm, casting a gentle glow that provided enough light for her to pray or journal, even during the night, without waking her husband.

While the dream replayed in her mind, she jotted it down as quickly as she could in her prayer journal. In the dream, she was both herself watching, and the girl in it. She was also able to perceive the thoughts of the people in the dream. Starting in a dark room, an unfinished basement perhaps—the floor was wet and dirty—she saw many children. She counted eight in the dim unnatural light of her dream but perceived many more in the shadows. The children were dressed in dirty camisoles and tap pants. They clustered together to stay warm and brave. They were young. Little even—some only six or seven.

In the dream, Beth was able to look around, and her eyes landed on the young woman in the center of the group. Maybe sixteen years old, with long hair, and fierce eyes. She was a warrior. She was holding a baby, wrapped in a blue blanket.

Beth paused her writing—*William*—her baby's face flashed in her mind as clearly as the day she brought him home from the hospital. His first smile, the way he cooed.

Forcing the memories, she wiped a tear from her eye and returned to the task at hand. The pain was still so tangible.

The guards came to the dream girl. "Let's go," they gruffly demanded.

Leaving no time for her to react, they grabbed her by the arms as she handed the infant to another girl. Beth noted the striking blue eyes of the baby as they tore the young girl from the group. She did not cry. She did not scream. Instead, she reassured the children. "It will be all right," she told them. "God will make a way. He will protect us."

She looked at them all directly. She did not avert her gaze. Her words were true.

The scene shifted and they hauled her up the stairs from what seemed to be a dungeon—rock wall, cement steps—as her dirty pajamas transformed into a hunter-green dress. It buttoned from the top collar all the way down. The dress ended below the knee, was fitted at the waist, and hugged her slight frame. Beth noted every detail because every detail remained clear in her mind.

The dreamer and child entered a cavernous room. A church of sorts. A sanctuary. Long wooden pews—covered in gray-blue fabric—lined the open area and stretched from the altar to a long row of windows and double glass doors. It was bright and sunshiny; the girl tried to shield her eyes as they adjusted to the light, which she had not seen in quite some time.

At the front of the room, standing behind an ornate oak podium stood a man in a blue plaid button-down shirt.

With all the blue imagery, Beth pulled out her phone and looked up what it meant spiritually. The answer was fitting: "Revelation."

The sanctuary was full of believers in this man. They had gathered to give him homage and worship the god he represented. But they did not worship the same God as Beth. No, not at all.

Beth surveyed their faces. She did not know these people. They say you don't dream of strangers, but although she could see several faces in detail, she did not know them.

Women and men were dressed in business suits. One woman—in a garnet-colored suit, with brown curly hair, an oval face, and bright eyes—swayed from side to side, hoping to receive a blessing from the man on the stage. Men in khaki slacks and button-downs like their leader watched with ravished smiles as the young woman stumbled into their pew.

Beth was astonished by the vivid details of the thoughts, complete with the intentions, of these dream people. Some of them knew of their leader's dark business. Most of them didn't. Strong men stood by the doors, looking ominous and angry, making sure no one came in—or got out. These evil men were fully aware and reaping the benefits of his dark game.

Beth drew an image in her journal that seemed to impress itself in her mind. A serpent in the center of a pentagram, carved into the altar and the side of every pew. She realized there was great evil represented in this dream. An evil she was being called to fight.

In the dream, Beth and the girl became one. The fear she felt was palpable as the man in the pulpit spoke to the congregation. He was looking directly at her. Panic started to rise in her throat. She looked about frantically for some face that might offer her help. They were all staring at the man. No one looked at her now. They were listening to every word that dripped off his lips.

He was coming. He was going down the stairs of the altar. Beth, one with the dream girl, froze. She had no idea what he would do, but terror spread through her entire body. When she looked up, he was there, standing in front of her. His dark eyes held her own. He seemed to respond to something in her eyes. Beth feared he somehow could *see her*. She could not move.

Beth became the observer again.

The man averted his gaze and reached out to touch the woman in the garnet suit. She let out a strange sound of awe and pain and crumpled into the pew. The girl, who willed herself to become invisible, avoided anything that might draw his attention. With her face forward and her body stiff, she was relieved yet still scared when he ignored her.

One thing Beth was certain of was that this girl was desperate for a way out and was finding none. The room was filled with adults, and yet not one of them said a word or offered help. She knew this was a dream but felt strongly that it represented a reality she did not want to consider.

Human trafficking.

There was much more detail to the dream, and she was able to review it as she wished; that was how real it was. She had no idea what it all meant.

Fields of Gomorrah

But it was important, so she tucked it away for the right time. She put down her pen as she considered the thoughts that were coming to her now—seeds planted in her mind that would take root as the Lord watered them. She would wait until He spoke again.

Until then, she would pray—fiercely—for this girl in the green dress.

Eighteen

Melody sat at the table in her kitchen. She drew the phone closer to her ear as the first ring sounded. She pondered the connection she and Beth had made over these last few months. They had met at church, but they didn't move in the same circles. They had a mutual friend but little else in common. Melody's children were older now; Beth's kids were elementary age.

While they had connected originally, they had not pursued an active friendship. Life was busy, after all. Over the last few years, they had met for coffee a few times. Maybe it was because they moved outside of each other's worlds that it came so easy to share everything. How often did people find a relationship they could trust that did not need to be nurtured daily? It seemed to Melody that this must be quite rare indeed.

Beth picked up on the second ring. "Hello, friend."

Melody could hear her smile. They were fellow truth seekers, and there would be some bit of information to dig into. It generally involved a topic that would require additional research. Their conversations were iron sharpening iron, and while they would always question the narrative due to their nature, they found themselves deeper in the Word to work out the details surrounding their thought-provoking questions.

"Hey, Beth! How are you and the family?"

After the niceties were accomplished, they moved on to some information Melody was eager to share.

"I was invited to attend a human trafficking awareness event last night," Melody began. "Do you know that roller skating rink on Tenth Avenue?"

"Yes, I took the kids there for a birthday party last month. It's like they're trying to revive the eighties! The girls had a blast. The place seems a little rundown, though."

"Well, I guess during the day it's okay, and there are many adults around then, but in the evenings maybe not so much. I learned it is affiliated with a prostitution ring. I really think we should be praying more intentionally for our community. This is an area with a high volume of trafficking. We've discussed it before, but I feel like it's becoming a focus, almost God-led." Melody shifted in her seat at the table.

"Yes! It's been on my mind as well," Beth agreed. "We should talk about it more—pray together at our Bible study this week."

"That's a great idea!" Melody was encouraged. "I'll see you then. Mae should be here as well."

Beth was happy to be with Melody in her kitchen, where Melody had prepared avocado toast with an egg over easy and coffee. Beth's girls were tutoring, and Mae would be arriving soon.

"So while we wait for Mae, I wanted to tell you something," Beth said tentatively, picking at the imaginary fuzz on her sweater.

"Go ahead," Melody encouraged.

"Well, I started to share with Billy how I opened up a little about William …" She faltered, feeling the tears fill her eyes. She cleared her throat and continued, "He still carries so much burden. I just saw the pain fresh in him as the morning we …" She couldn't finish the sentence.

"Oh, Beth, I'm so sorry." Melody's brow furrowed, and she took Beth's hand in hers. "I can't imagine the grief you carry."

"I just feel like, sometimes, maybe God doesn't hear me. He doesn't see my pain." The tears fell from her eyes now, and she wiped them with the back of her hand. She drank slowly from her coffee, hoping to distract her heart from her mind.

"I know. I have been there." Melody moved to grab a box of Kleenex from the counter and set it in front of Beth. "When the prayer hits the ceiling and falls back down. Doesn't seem to get anywhere, and you don't feel God the same way."

Beth set her cup down and nodded as she wiped her eyes with a tissue. "Exactly."

Pulling her Bible near, Melody flipped through it. "Here, listen—Psalm 22:24 tells us this: 'For he hath not despised nor abhorred the affliction of the afflicted; neither hath he hid his face from him; but when he cried unto him, he heard.'" Flipping a page or two over, she continued. "And Psalm 30:5 assures us that weeping may endure for the night, but joy comes in the morning."

"Hmmm." Beth shook her shoulders. "Some nights are longer than others." She offered a slight shrug.

Melody patted her hand again. "That is so true. But here, Psalm 34:18—"

"The LORD is close to the brokenhearted," Beth quoted, "and saves those who are crushed in spirit." Although she smiled, she couldn't shake the sadness from her eyes. "He gave me that verse in the days that followed William's death."

They heard a quick knock, followed by the swish of the door opening. "Hello, ladies!" Mae called from the hall, energetic and boisterous as ever.

Sharing a laugh with Beth, Melody responded. "We are in the kitchen, Mae. Come on in."

Beth dried her eyes and opened the Bible in front of her. "You were going to tell us about the human trafficking event you went to, Melody."

"Oh, that sounds interesting." Mae's eyes lit up as she filled a chair with her bags and sat in the one next to it while Melody poured her a cup of coffee.

"It really was more about how God is pulling this to my attention. It feels like I've been placed on a mission to target this tragic industry in prayer!"

"Well, it's quite interesting to me, because the other night I had the most intense dream." Beth shared. "There was a young woman and a baby wrapped in a blue blanket ..." Her voice cracked, but she continued. "There was so much detail. A man in the pulpit in a blue flannel shirt. Blue pews lined a vast room, and they were filled by people from all walks of life. The girl was dragged from a basement room up some dungeon-like stairs and forced to stand in the room."

"Oh my," Mae's coffee cup was poised halfway to her lips. "Was this a dream or a vision?"

"I don't know, Mae, because it was like I was there." She proceeded to describe the rest of the dream in full detail to her friends.

"The dream was so real—even if the girl wasn't, she certainly represents thousands of women and children, even men, who are trafficked across the world. This really ties in to what you're talking about, Melody. And I get that this atrocity exists, but what can we do about it?" Beth despaired. "I mean, it's everywhere. People in our neighborhoods are probably worshipping Satan outright. The satanic elite has been focused on genocide under the guise of helping women since their inception, and now let's add human trafficking to our town." She paused to catch her breath. "How do housewives make a difference in all this insanity?"

Mae answered, "I know how." She slapped her hands against the wooden table, emphasizing her point. "We pray."

She looked at her friends. "Listen, I know it sounds simplistic, but the truth often is. It's just our own minds that want to complicate and convolute it. If we truly knew the power that is accessible through prayer and how the Lord can move in our midst when we become willing vessels ... well, I think we would take Thessalonians a little more seriously and truly pray without ceasing!"

Melody nodded, smiling. "I have to share something with you both." She set down her coffee cup. "About six months ago, Mae and I did a study on the power and purpose of prayer. Since then, I have been diligent in my prayer time and the Lord has been revealing many things to me—in the last couple of months, since we've gotten together, Beth." Melody tapped her fingers against the table as if she'd just made this connection. "Interesting.

Anyway, since we reconnected, I've been praying, and toward the end of the prayer, one word kind of materializes in my mind."

"That's fascinating." Beth ran a finger around the rim of her coffee cup.

Melody retrieved her journal from her large purse. After flipping through the pages, she turned the book so the ladies could read along with her. "March, with her, restriction—demarcation. What do you think it means?"

Mae took a moment and leaned back in her chair. "Well, considering what God is awakening in your spirit regarding trafficking, I can see how all of these things connect. March—that sounds like an order, right? Like a calling?"

She looked at Beth and Melody. They both nodded.

"Yes, that is exactly what I was thinking!" Melody added.

"With her," Beth offered, leaning forward in her chair. "Could be the girl in my dream or the people she represents."

"Restriction. Demarcation. Restriction …" Mae played with the last two words. "It could be that the enemy is restricted. In the physical realm, that is human trafficking. And the likes of Draven Wolfe and the other global elites. Demarcation—could be the enemy has marked his territory."

"Or we mark ours." Melody tagged on with a broad smile.

Mae's face was set like a flint. Beth was eager to hear what she was thinking. "We are definitely onto something here, girls," Mae said, again striking the table for emphasis.

Melody's voice rose with excitement. "You know I have wanted to be a part of something extraordinary for a long time. For years, I prayed to God to give me a glimpse of the supernatural. Let me be used by Him. Something, anything."

"And here we are." Mae's smile broke across her face.

"Oh boy," Beth mumbled. "What can we possibly do to fight something as big as human trafficking and global elites? I barely know anything about either."

"Well, it starts with prayer," Mae assured her. "And we can all do that!"

Nineteen

They came in the night and took Missy away. While time did not exist here, Cassie did the best she could by counting meals and the times they were told to sleep. Based on that, she guessed it had been at least two days. Before Missy had been taken, there had been glimpses of the wounded, angry child living inside her. She was often moody, sometimes jealous, and occasionally violent. But she was the closest thing Cassie had to a friend here, and she helped with the little kids. Cassie was worried she wouldn't return.

Three children piled around Cassie's lap. Realizing these kids were just the tip of an unseen iceberg, Cassie began to see a larger picture and glimpse her purpose. The wind whipped outside the rectangle room with the noisy discontent of traffic. Cassie noted the car horns and revving engines. It was a city, but she had no idea which one. The thought burdened her. They were stuck in the middle of a bustling metropolis, and no one knew they were there.

When the door opened, the guards shoved Missy toward the kids.

"Get your hands off me, you filthy pigs," she demanded. "I *came* to Ethan, you idiots. I *chose* to work here. I'll be in charge of all this before long!"

"Right," said Melvin, his voice filled with disgust as he sized her up. "You mighta *chose* to come in, but you don't get to choose when to leave. He called for you once, that doesn't mean a thing. You're here now and you're as stuck as the rest of them." He pointed his chin in Cassie's general direction.

Missy spat in his face.

"Listen, Mel. Melvin." She was taunting him.

Cassie's jaw dropped at her show of impudence. Whether brave, stupid, or desperate, none of those attitudes brought good choices.

"I'm not the cattle." Missy nodded toward the children. "I'm a *worker*." She stressed the last word as though it had greater meaning.

Amber grabbed Melvin's arm in mid-swing, blocking a blow of angry retaliation. "We don't touch the merchandise for no good reason." She stated this simply, devoid of any compassion or acknowledgment that the "merchandise" were children.

The two guards left the room, but not before Melvin made a threatening gesture at Missy. She didn't flinch and she didn't back down.

Cassie walked over to where she stood. Missy's eyes were cold as ice, her face set like stone. Cassie faltered a little. This did not feel like the same girl who had looked out for her and comforted the children since their arrival. Cassie, met by hate and anger seething in Missy, took a step back as Missy locked eyes on her.

"What do you want?" she demanded, her chest heaving.

"I was … I was coming to see if you were okay," Cassie stammered.

"You're checking on me?" She scoffed. "Like we're on the playground?" She laughed bitterly. "Maybe … maybe you want to welcome me into your home?" She made a broad sweeping gesture with her arms, turning in a slow circle. "Well, what a great place you've got here. Thanks for having me over."

In a flash, she was inches from Cassie's face. Her dark eyes blazed with fury. Startled, Cassie let out a small cry.

"Don't talk to me. Don't look at me," Missy whispered vehemently. "Get this—we are not *friends*. I don't want anything to do with any of you scum. Got it? I'm here cuz it's better than what's out there." She gestured with her hand toward the door and then back at the floor of the rectangle room. She stepped back and turned away, then finished her rant. "I doubt you can say the same. So save it."

Shaking, Cassie returned to the children. She tried to soothe her erratic breathing and calm the trembling in her hands. She didn't know what to think of the girl's sudden change of character—except that maybe there were two of them.

Several hours later, Missy had returned to normal. Well, mostly normal. Cassie couldn't remember what normal was, anyway. But one thing had become an obvious change; Missy was very interested in the attention that James gave Cassie.

Cassie pieced together the hierarchy, even in a place like this. Missy expected to be the one in charge here. Keeping her at arm's length, Cassie tried her best to observe, to try to understand what the change was. She could not pinpoint it. But for the moment, the Missy she had first met was here—crying and alone in the corner. Missy did not stir as Cassie tiptoed over to her. She didn't know how Missy would receive her.

Missy looked up through eyes that brimmed with tears. "It's okay, Cassie. It's … me."

"What do you mean, Missy?" Cassie asked softly and took a seat next to her.

Missy shrugged. "Sometimes, I hear voices. I don't always know who I am, or if I'm even here." She looked at Cassie and then away. "You wouldn't understand."

"You can still talk to me about it," Cassie offered.

Missy shifted and ran her palms down her legs. She took a deep breath. "It started a couple years ago. I was in this foster home, and they were abusive. I guess I pushed it all out of my mind, 'cause I don't remember much. But I ran away, and when the cops picked me up, the agency decided I should go see the shrink. Dr. Phillips."

She turned to face Cassie. "She was a bit of a freak. Everything she wore was black, her dress, shoes, glasses. Even her hair was jet-black. And she was so pale. Man, when I first saw her, I thought she was a ghost. It creeped me out, but they wouldn't listen. The adults … they said it was the best thing for me. I didn't have a choice."

Cassie nodded, carefully listening and piecing together the things she was saying with the things she clearly wasn't.

"So I had to see her cuz when they found me, I was all cut up. My arms, my legs, my stomach." Missy looked away now and absently rubbed her midsection.

"You don't have to relive it, Missy. If it's too hard—" Cassie hoped to ease some of the girl's pain.

"Yeah, I know." Missy offered a weak smile but pressed on. "So this doctor did some hypnosis therapy on me. But when I was under ... it was scary."

Cassie placed a tentative arm around Missy, encouraging her to go on.

"I met this kid in my mind. I can't really explain it, I can only tell it." Her brow was furrowed, her palms rubbing with new intensity against her legs. "I met this kid. Said his name was Ahriman. He looked harmless, wearing white shorts and a tank top. We walked in this field, by a pond. He introduced a friend of his to me. Renata. She seemed to appear out of nowhere.

"She had on a white dress. A big blue bow held back some curls. She was cute. Till she smiled. Rows of teeth." Missy started to tremble, as a tear slid down her cheek. "'She's your spirit guide,' Ahriman said. 'She'll take care of you.' He said it like it was good. But it felt bad." She took in a deep ragged breath.

"Anyway, I don't remember what happened next, but since then, I hear her in my head." Missy grimaced, turned her head away from Cassie, and seemed to zone out. When she returned to Cassie and the real world, her eyes had dulled, and her expression was blank. Cassie slowly pulled her arm away, feeling a sudden chill. "Renata wants you to leave."

Cassie began to argue when Missy snarled. Baring her teeth, a low guttural sound coming from her throat, she made sharp, erratic motions toward Cassie. Instinctively, Cassie backed away, wishing she had a large stick. She retreated to the other side of the room.

The familiar screech of the door echoed in the room, and James stood in the doorway. His slight build was a silhouette against the light behind him. He had an awkward, unlearned way about him, and Cassie knew it was him before she could see his face. She wondered if he had ever been to school or around girls at all, and how he got here—in the midst of this "business."

He was the weaker brother, both in mind and body. As he limped across the room, each child lifted their dirty bowl, and he dropped clumps of oatmeal into each one from an old banged-up pot. He smiled as he came close to Cassie, his brown hair falling into his face in a way that made James Dean look cool but made James Walker look unkempt.

Kneeling beside Cassie, he filled the bowl without taking his eyes away from her. It was disconcerting. She shuddered and turned her face.

"I have some news." He had a big, stupid grin on his face. It caused her heart to drop to her stomach. Her palms began to sweat.

"W-what news, James?" she stammered.

"Ethan said I can have you. You are gonna be mine when you're done with the business."

He sounded so excited. She wanted to vomit. *Have me? Done with the business?* Before she realized what she was doing, her hand had acted of its own accord and slapped him across the face. She let out a gasp. In shock, his hand flew to his cheek where it was already showing a bright pink. His smile was gone.

"I am not property, James!" Instantly regretting her decision, and realizing she had gone too far, she began to apologize. Obviously, she *was* a commodity.

His madness was hereditary. How could anyone fight that?

"I'm sorry, James!" She backpedaled as fast as she could to soothe his wounded ego. He had actually meant that as a gift, a privilege he could bestow upon any one of them in this room. But he chose Cassie, and she should be honored.

She would be his. His property. His trophy. Her stomach turned, but she held down the bile. However, she would be on the other side of this horrific nightmare. The one helping to capture kids? Or maybe she would be bringing the oatmeal to future victims. Never!

"Of course, that would be amazing." She gritted the words out through a hard smile. "Being your girl sounds like a dream come true."

His idiot grin returned, even as his hand rubbed his cheek. He set down the pot and rummaged in the pocket of his oversize tan jacket.

"Here," he handed her a small book.

A gentle smile softened Cassie's expression as she took the gift. A Bible.

Missy let out a throttled yell through clenched teeth. Cassie and James both turned in her direction. She was glaring at them. Her face was mottled and red, and her hands were in tight balls at her sides.

"You?" She turned her full attention to Cassie. "You? He chose you?"

Cassie did not know what to think. She didn't fully realize why Missy was upset or what any of this meant. She certainly was not thrilled that James had *chosen* her. It was a life sentence for Cassie. She didn't want to be *owned*. She wanted to be *free*.

Twenty

Billy picked up the phone and dialed the number of Talia Wilson, the young mother he'd spoken to at the park. He opened his notebook and clicked the pen.

She picked up on the third ring, sounding breathless.

"Miss Wilson." Billy nodded at Dixon when he entered the room. Billy hadn't seen him in four days, and now he came strolling in with his shirt untucked and hair shaggy and uncombed. "This is Detective Everett. We met at the playground last week."

"Oh, yeah. Hello, Detective." Her voice faded in and out. He could hear the baby crying in the background.

"Is this a good time? I have a couple of follow-up questions." He repeatedly clicked his ballpoint pen. He avoided the glare coming from his partner. Dixon leaned against Billy's desk. Apparently, he wasn't going anywhere.

"Sorry, no, it's good … umm. It's nap time. We just walked in from the library. Give me a minute."

She was gone. She must have set the phone down because Billy could still hear the distant sound of crying and soft words from Talia. After a few moments, he heard a door close and shuffling noises. Finally, Talia returned.

"Hey, yeah. Sorry 'bout that. She's a holy terror if she doesn't get her nap," Talia explained. "Questions?"

"Yes." Billy decided to get right to it, though he did turn his back on Dixon. He appreciated Talia's direct approach. "When Rocky was with the little boy, did he mention anything that the kid said or what games they played?"

"Let me think." Billy heard tapping, like manicured nails on a wood table. "Um, yeah. There was something about a friend he was gonna take Rocky to meet. They played Rescue Dogs ... some game about hero dogs. And that Rocky would be a star if he would go with him."

"You said he wanted to take him to a friend. Did he mention any names?"

"Well, he's little, but he said something ... what was it? It wasn't a name and definitely not his normal words." She was talking more to herself than to Billy. "Ah, I can't remember." Her focus seemed to return. "But his puppy superpower was concerning—it was invisibility. Which is normal, but he was only invisible to adults. And he told Rocky his job would be to tickle people as an invisible dog."

"Thank you, Mrs. Wilson. You've been a great help. If I think of any other questions, can I call you?"

"You bet. Whatever I can do to help catch these losers and get that little girl back. I'm just so thankful Rocky is safe, ya know?"

"Yes, I am too." Billy tapped his pen against his notebook, disappointed there wasn't more to go on.

"Potential!" Talia exclaimed. "The kid told Rocky he had 'human potential.' Rocky hardly knew how to say the word."

"Okay, that's good." He straightened in his chair as he wrote down the two words. "Thank you, Mrs. Wilson. Have a good day." Billy ended the call. Turning back to his desk, he picked up his file and his coffee cup and stood to leave.

"Excuse me," Dixon stood in his way. "I thought we agreed we were done with this case."

Billy's answer was simple and direct. "No. We didn't." He pressed past Dixon without waiting for a response. A host of doubts were confirmed.

Twenty-One

Cassie had to believe there was a purpose for this pain, some meaning in the madness. Struggling to find it, she drifted into a dream like none she had ever had.

She found herself in a sanctuary. The pews filled the back of the room while a massive stage consumed the front. The vast room was filled with men and women who were worshipping the man on the stage. He was large and well-dressed. Not a hair out of place, yet the sweat on his brow and upper lip revealed his humanity. She knew him. He had been to the rectangle room where she was kept. Ethan brought him in and was nervous in his presence. Ethan was never nervous.

In this dream, there were two women she had never seen before. And although the entire room was filled with strangers, these two looked directly at her. They could see her. Instantly, she was filled with great hope.

The scene shifted, and now Cassie was in a forest. The grass was scarce, and the moss was lush on the north side of the trees. As she walked along an avenue of soft fallen pine needles, the path brought her to a large flat rock and a small cave.

Cassie climbed up and rested on the rock. Sunlight pierced through the canopy of leaves above, and she was tenderly warmed by its rays. She was alone for a blessed moment. Safe. Here she had no scars, no terror. She found peace in this place.

It seemed that hours had passed when some rustling in the bushes roused her. Out of the brambles lumbered two she-bears with their cubs. Panicked, she started to back up higher onto the rock. The cubs followed close behind their mamas. The group spotted Cassie on the rock and paused. Snorting in her direction, they returned their focus to their mischievous cubs. Cassie concluded they felt she was no threat as the two bears collapsed to the ground with a large thump that blew pine needles and leaves across the ground. The cubs came close, and the mama bears attempted to clean them as they played.

Tentatively, Cassie crawled down from the rock—so curious about these animals and how they were looking after their babies. Bravely, she closed the gap and approached the small family, longing to be protected and cared for the same way. It reminded her vividly of her mother's unfailing love.

She held out a hand, palm down, to one of the mama bears—the only trick she knew for greeting an animal. The creature was light brown in color and her round brown eyes looked at Cassie. The bear responded by rolling her body against the ground. It seemed to be an invitation, so Cassie came closer and sat down near her. Leaning back against her warm body and snuggling down against her colossal shaggy side, she found comfort in feeling the beast's breath rise and fall. The bear draped one paw across the child's body, her fierce claws a threat not to Cassie but to others. Cassie would not wager against the she-bear. Resting in the security of her embrace, Cassie was suddenly reminded of the way her mother held her. She felt the woman's presence, confident that at that very moment, her mother was praying.

Waking with a start, she was greeted by the hostile darkness of the room. It stole what little hope the dream had provided. The warmth she had felt in the presence of the she-bear evaporated as reality returned and she felt the cold steel floor of the rectangle room. Allowing only a few tears now, she took comfort in knowing the dream was from God. She retrieved the Bible James had brought her, hoping the delicate pages would bring her some comfort.

She opened the Bible and nearly gasped in disbelief! In the darkness, the very darkness she knew would steal away any chance to actually read the Word, the book in her hand glowed with a strange and soft blue light.

Slamming the Bible abruptly, she dragged the room frantically with her eyes to see if anyone had been awakened. Slowly, she turned to her favorite scripture, Psalm 18. Imagery flew off the page—"In my distress I called upon the Lord, and cried unto my God: he heard my voice out of his temple, and my cry came before him, even into his ears."

"Fire out of his mouth devoured," she continued on with great hope as she read the next lines. "He bowed the heavens also, and came down ... he did fly upon the wings of the wind."

Further still, "He sent out his arrows, and scattered them." She muffled a laugh as she read through the faithful words of a rescuing God.

This miracle was what she needed to forge ahead. This supernatural commitment rang as a reminder of who was fighting this battle for her. She might not have been able to see the angels she knew were there to protect her, but she felt the demons. She felt them tremble as her hushed whispers lifted the holy words off the page and to the Father. The tide was turning.

She found the pen James had brought her days ago and scribbled furiously in the margins of the leather-bound book, noting every detail she could think of. Kids' names, where they were from, the clients, what they looked like—any detail that she thought could possibly help bring some justice and closure once she was free from this nightmare.

Once her mind was exhausted of every detail, she turned to the front pages of the book. She noted the inscription on the first page:

> For my boys, Ethan and James. Read this book together.
> Stay close.
> Love, Mama

Considering what that meant, she felt maybe God was working even in the heart of her captors. If that was possible? Turning back to Psalms now, she began to softly read aloud. Lily came over and crawled into her lap. Resting her weary head against Cassie's chest, she listened intently as Cassie read from the Psalms. Lily didn't react to the blue light. Cassie smiled, concluding that it truly was just for her.

"Psalm 18 is all about how God came to rescue His child," Cassie explained. "It's like a hero's adventure. The imagery is fierce. 'At the brightness that was before him his thick clouds passed, hail stones and coals of fire.' And here, 'He brought me forth also into a large place.'"

Lily turned her head up and just smiled.

Cassie smiled back. "I'm from Florida and never saw a hailstone. The concept of ice falling from the sky is amazing."

Lily murmured, "I wish God would send a storm here. And it could sweep us away from here. I'd rather be Dorothy and wind up in Oz. I'm scared, Cassie. And I want to go home." She pressed her little face against Cassie's chest and wept.

Cassie felt her own tears fall in response. When would this nightmare end?

Twenty-Two

At the precinct, Billy waited for Dixon to arrive from his assignment. His schedule had been erratic of late, and he was seldom at the office. Billy needed to know what Dixon had learned from a lead they had picked up from Talia Wilson. After a quick search, Billy had connected Rocky's words to a corporation run by the up-and-coming Ethan Walker, a savvy thirty-something. Little else was revealed on the website, so Dixon was supposed to go speak with some people to learn more about it.

The precinct was a bustle of activity. Detectives like Billy were combing through details and doing research. On the other side of their glassed-in offices, the phones were ringing off the hook as the front desk clerks tried to keep up. The public came and went, making various requests in the front lobby.

As he waited, Billy sorted through the contents of the case file. He grabbed a pen from the cup to his right and pulled his notebook from the top right drawer. He began searching for any connection he might have missed and how it might tie to Human Potential and Ethan Walker. Lily was taken from the playground nearly three months ago. The leads were getting buried, and time was running out.

He leafed through all the papers and photos, realizing her picture was missing.

After moving to the desk across from him, Billy rummaged through the paperwork and trash that littered his partner's space. As different as he could be from his new partner, Billy had struggled to form a bond with him in the past year. Dixon was sharp-tongued, lazy, and unreliable. His life was in a state of chaos, reflected in the disarray he lived in. Billy moved candy wrappers, chip bags, and half-full coffee cups into the trash bin. He picked up notes written on scrap paper. *Clark 12:30 Sports bar. Dentist 8:00 Tuesday.* Billy found pages pulled from various case files and a business card from the Wisdom Foundation.

The Wisdom Foundation? Billy paused his search. Was Dixon connected to the Wisdom Foundation? With the card in his hand, Billy pushed around a few more layers of paper until he caught a glimpse of Lily's face, blue eyes shining up at him. He picked the photo out of the mess and took both picture and card back to his own desk.

He stuck the image back into the case file and then stared at the business card. Leaning back in his chair, he examined the few details that the card provided. Quite simplistic, it was a black card with white font of the company name and a single tagline—"unlocking your potential." A glance at the back told him it was blank. He turned it back over and caught a detail in the light. In a shade slightly darker than the card base was the circle image he had discovered on the website. This one was more detailed. Definitely a serpent in a circle devouring its own tail. *When did Dixon make this connection, and how did he come across the card? Had he visited them already? Why would he do that and not tell me—or have me go with him?*

Billy quickly placed the card in his top drawer as he heard Dixon stumble into the room. He wore dark jeans, a white dress shirt with a blazer, and sunglasses.

"Hey, Billy!" he called out. "It was a bust. No one shared anything of interest. No connection there, partner."

Observing him closely, Billy decided to ask about the Wisdom Foundation. "Got it. Are you gonna take those shades off? What have you heard about the Wisdom Foundation?"

Dixon's sunglasses hid his eyes, and if Billy hadn't been watching, he would have missed that his face fell—but only for a moment.

"Um, yeah. I think so. Some New Age church or something. They have a few locations here in the city."

Dixon took off his blazer, set it on the back of his chair, and then nervously unbuttoned his sleeves and pushed them up his forearms. He would not look Billy in the face. He busied himself at the desk, not even seeming to realize that Billy had touched anything.

"So where does that leave us?" he asked, still not taking off the sunglasses. "Ready to close this down?"

Billy caught a glimpse of a fresh tattoo on the inside of Dixon's left wrist. A snake eating its own tail. "What's that?" Billy stood and leaned against his desk so he could face Dixon.

"Oh, just a new addition." He smiled. The flesh was pink around the edges of the serpent.

"Does it mean anything?" Billy's interest was sincere.

Dixon removed his sunglasses, revealing a large black eye.

"Whoa—what happened?" Billy let out a low whistle. "Who were you fighting?"

Dixon laughed. "My old lady." He set the glasses down in the mess and began to rummage through his filing system. "Hey, I had the photo of the Chamberlain girl here, have you seen it?" Dixon looked over at his partner, eyes narrowed.

"Yeah, I found it in all that garbage. Seriously, you need to clean up here. It's a mess." Billy turned back to his desk and picked up the folder. "I don't suggest pulling items out of the case file, Dixon. It's why we have a file."

Dixon stood up, his hands on his hips and his shoulders hunched forward. "You went through my things, man?"

Billy looked up at him, surprised at the level of anger. "Yeah, I had to find the photo for the file. What's it matter? You think you have a secure filing system over there?"

"Listen, you don't go through my desk. We may be partners, but keep your hands off my things. Got it?"

Billy raised both hands and shook his head, "Yeah, man. I got it. I'll respect it if you don't pull key documents out of the file."

"If you're looking for something, then ask." His voice was climbing and drawing the attention of their peers.

"Can't ask if I can't find you. Calm down, Dixon. I hear you. Do you hear me?" Billy refused to back down. Dixon was now leaning over his desk, his eyes bulging, his face red.

"I hear you," he said, his voice a low threat. "Just make sure you don't do it again." He grabbed his blazer and stormed back out the door.

Billy shook his head, his speculations confirmed. His partner was in something over his head. Billy was going to find out what that was exactly.

Twenty-Three

The guards brought broken children back from misery, and Cassie was the one to tend to them. The oldest in the room, she became the caregiver, praying over each child. Holding and rocking them. Singing over them. Songs that she remembered her mother singing to her. That life seemed light-years away now.

Mom, I wish I could see you. I wish you could hold me. Her throat tightened as she fought back the thought. "There's a tear in your eye, and I'm wondering why." She sang the Irish lullaby to the little one in her lap.

Inevitably, tears would flow. From Cassie and the children. Irish eyes and African American and Chinese. They were an international pool of choices. She cringed, feeling her heart break again and again.

Lily was in her arms now, blond hair splayed against Cassie's arm as the child rested against her chest. "It was a leader of some sort today, Cassie," she whimpered. "He had a strange tattoo on his wrist." She touched the inside of her right wrist as she spoke, but her eyes were dazed, looking straight ahead as if she were desperately trying to forget what else had happened in that room.

"A cobra, I think," she continued. "I remember seeing one in a book at school. It was in a circle trying to eat its own tail." She wiggled, probably to shift the memory in her mind to stay focused on the tattoo and not the man.

"He kept saying he was a master. And he demanded that I bow. Do you think Jesus will be mad at me because I bowed?" She picked at her grubby nails. Guards demanded the children wash their bodies, but they never paid attention to the details. Cassie doubted their spirits would ever be clean again.

One of Cassie's customers had gotten out of control, giving her a swollen eye and split lip. She shifted Lily over to her other side so she could better see her face. In fact, he had a similar tattoo and was the reason Cassie had asked the kids to start paying attention.

"You only bowed in your body, Lily bear. You didn't bow in your heart." Cassie kept back the sob that threatened to break through, though a tear fell from her swollen eye. "Jesus will help us. I don't know how, but when it happens, we will know it is Him."

I want to believe, Jesus. Please help my doubt. I just don't see a way out. Only You can free us. Only You can save us.

"Nobody is coming for us," Missy called out from across the room, where she sat against the wall with her hands on her knees and anger-filled eyes staring directly at Cassie.

Even in the darkness, the look sent a chill down Cassie's spine. She responded, chin set and voice firm, "You can't know that, Missy."

Slowly and awkwardly, as though her limbs were not quite connected to her body, Missy crawled across the room to Cassie. Pure reflex pushed Cassie against the wall as her arms shielded the child in her lap. Missy, or whatever was controlling her, stopped inches from Cassie's face.

"You can't know that they are, either," Missy sneered in a low throaty whisper. Almost as if something was using her vocal cords.

"Well, I can hope. I can pray," Cassie stated, though her confidence was shaken, and her words faltered.

"Hmmph," Missy scoffed, her voice back to normal, and she settled in next to Cassie. "Sure, you can. Fat lot of good that does."

The words pierced Cassie's heart. They reflected on what she knew she was struggling with. *Please help my unbelief, Lord.* Lily slipped away as quickly as she could, and Cassie put a bit of distance between herself and Missy.

"Anyway, what did James bring you the other day?" Missy shifted gears, her eyes narrowing in suspicion.

"Just a Bible."

Missy burst out in laughter, slapping her knee. "A Bible? Ha! That's hilarious! What on earth would you want that for?"

Cassie held herself together and leveled her gaze at Missy. "You can mock me, but it doesn't change what I believe."

Missy's laughter slowed. Her countenance changed. Cassie shivered; it seemed a different person took over Missy at that moment. The moment was fleeting, and her friend softened.

"I'm sorry, Cassie. You're right. I shouldn't poke fun. It's hard enough in here without having something to hope for. It's just that hope is dangerous in a place like this. It's deceitful, and when help never comes, the crash you feel as hope dies ... it's so devastating."

Cassie realized she was sincere. Maybe she was speaking from personal experience. Cassie would hold on to her faith, for sure. Yet she feared there was some truth in Missy's words. "Have you ever read the Bible, Missy?"

"I had a foster mom that did." She busied herself with a loose string on her shirt. "She read it out loud to us every night. Sometimes it sounded like music to me. I liked the stories. David and Goliath were cool. I think there are some giants I would like to slay." She trailed off.

"That's true. I like the idea of sitting in a pit around a bunch of lions like Daniel did ... It's really kind of what we are in now." The revelation sank into Cassie's mind. "Yeah, we are in a pit, and we are surrounded by lions."

"Yeah, but these lions bite," Lily tentatively scooted close to Cassie again, keeping a wary eye on Missy.

"God is still with us," Cassie said. "He is fighting for us, even when we can't see Him." She ran her fingers through Lily's soft hair, comforting her. Soon the little one fell asleep.

Missy and Cassie continued their conversation into the night. Cassie shared some of her favorite verses. As sleep drew near, her mind grew fuzzy, and she dropped her guard.

"Missy, I think I'm late." Cassie spoke and knew immediately it was a mistake. The Missy she had been talking with for hours disappeared in front of her eyes and was replaced by the terrifying replica of her friend.

"Late." An evil grin spread slowly across Missy's face, never reaching her eyes. "That means they will take you from here. Give you an abortion. Free you from the parasite." She giggled in a way that made Cassie's skin crawl.

Oh, why did I say that out loud? And to her? I never know which Missy I'm going to get. A mental issue is as plain as my nose, and I still trusted her? What is wrong with me? Why do I make such poor choices?

Cassie closed her eyes. Groaning inwardly, she felt the anxiety descend upon her like a blanket. Wrapped in fear, she said without much hope, "Please don't share that, Missy."

"Of course not." Still, she smiled. "Who would I tell?" And she crawled back to her spot against the wall.

Twenty-four

Beth and the girls arrived at the pediatric office for her appointment with Dr. Morrison. They were greeted by the same nurse who helped her at the last appointment, who led them back to the exam room shortly after checking in.

"We are so glad you are giving us a second chance on a first impression," the nurse smiled warmly. She opened the door and walked them into the small room, identical to the one before.

"My pleasure," Beth replied. "We really have heard so many positive things about your facility. I know that even pediatricians are not one size fits all."

The girls settled onto the padded bench as they waited for the doctor to arrive. They did not have long to wait. A soft knock sounded on the door, followed by the doctor entering. He was in his forties with a cartoon character tie, and his warm smile and calm demeanor were a complete change from their initial experience.

The girls visibly relaxed. Their tight shoulders softened. Maggie let out a sigh, and Esther began to chatter. This was all the confirmation Beth needed. She was so comfortable she didn't realize the door was still slightly open.

Dr. Morrison started with easy, get-to-know-you questions. "Do you girls play any sports?"

"I like softball," Esther announced, pretending to swing a bat and almost falling off the exam table.

"Whoa there." Beth intercepted her, helping reposition the child. They all laughed.

Just then, Beth looked up and caught a glimpse of Dr. Clark in the open crack of the door. She could see the harsh expression glaring back at her.

Beth's face must have shown her discomfort, for Dr. Morrison addressed it right away. "Is everything okay, Mrs. Everett? You look concerned." He turned his eyes to see what she was looking at, but Dr. Clark had moved away from the door.

"Oh, w-well." Beth stumbled. "It was that doctor. From before. I just feel so uncomfortable. I do have one question." She shifted slightly in her seat. "Can I request not to be scheduled with her? I know it's a personal thing—every family is different. It's just something I would be more comfortable having arranged."

"Of course," Dr. Morrison agreed with a straight face. She couldn't tell if her request bothered him, or if he agreed with her misgivings. Either way, she was glad it was all arranged. "I'll make a note in the charts of both girls. Well, it was very nice to meet you. I look forward to seeing you again on your well-check visit. Feel free to schedule that whenever it is convenient."

He stood and held out his hand to Beth, who shook it. Then he turned and saluted both girls in a dramatic effect. Maggie and Esther looked at each other and giggled.

Stopping at the desk to schedule the well-check visits, Beth felt the hairs on the back of her neck rise. She tried to shake off the feeling, but when she looked up, she saw Dr. Clark staring at Esther. She pulled the girls closer to her and stared defiantly at the physician.

With her chin up and her lips a thin line, Beth demanded, "Can I help you with something, Dr. Clark?"

Dr. Clark's eyes moved from child to parent, narrowing slightly, while a slow smirk spread across her face. "No, Mrs. Everett. You ladies have a good day."

"I'll call back to schedule the appointments with Dr. Morrison. Have a good day," Beth said to the receptionist. She gathered her chicks close to her side and hustled out of the office, seriously considering whether she could bring her children here again. She loved the staff, and Dr. Morrison was wonderful—but Dr. Clark. Beth shivered. The woman filled her with apprehension.

Twenty-Five

Billy leaned back in his chair, stretching his body and rubbing his neck. From the window, a man caught his eye, having what seemed to be a heated conversation with himself. Billy took note of the way he limped. The hoodie drawn tight around his face kept any features from Billy's sharp eye. But the cold wind of the day brought bits of snow that struck down like pellets from the sky and he pulled his jacket tighter. Billy lost sight of him when he rounded the corner, passing by the station.

It was a good time for a coffee break, Billy decided as he pushed back from the desk. Stretching his legs as he walked toward the coffee pot was a welcome relief. He had been at his desk for three hours and was still not any closer to a lead. He felt the frustration building.

What was the connection between Ethan Walker and Draven Wolfe? What was he to make of the serpent image? Was it all connected? The questions continued to race through his mind as he filled a paper cup with the dark liquid.

Looking up from the rim of the coffee cup, Billy watched with interest as the limping man entered the building and spoke with the front desk attendant. *He passed the building. He must have circled back.* The man seemed agitated as he spoke with the female officer. Billy couldn't quite make out the words. She handed the man a notepad, and his hands gestured wildly, calming only enough to write something quickly. He abruptly turned and rushed as fast as his bum leg would let him out the door.

Billy walked over to the attendant. "Hey, Leslie," he asked as she swiveled her chair to face him. "What was that about?"

Fields of Gomorrah

"Crazy. He went all nuts saying he wanted to leave an anonymous tip. I told him fine, but then he seemed to talk himself out of it." She shrugged her shoulders and lifted her hands. "Then he asked for a piece of paper, and I handed that to him. He scratched something down, but it doesn't make sense to me." She turned back to her desk and picked up the crumpled paper. "Here," she said, handing it to him. "Maybe it will help one of you guys back there."

Billy took the note from Leslie and headed back to his desk. When he saw the drawing the man with the limp had scrawled on the page, he realized instantly it was a tie to his case. It was a roughly drawn image of the serpent biting its tail followed by two words: "shipping containers."

He grabbed the case folder and walked to the chief's office.

A modest office for a magnanimous man, the space belied its occupant's importance. Chief Greg Stone had been in the field for nearly thirty years and had solved numerous cases that most men would have filed away. He was tenacious and driven. His office was simple with a desk and leather chair, two chairs opposite the desk. Windows covered three walls like a cubicle built into the center of the vast room. The wall behind him held nothing but a few accolades and accomplishments.

Tossing the crumpled paper on Chief Stone's desk, Billy said, "Are you familiar with that symbol?" He walked to the glass wall overlooking the rows of desks of the detectives. He set the file down next to him as he leaned against the low file cabinet.

The chief picked up his reading glasses from a stack of papers on his desk. Holding the picture, he studied it for a few seconds. "Definitely resembles the images from the slide." He took a sip of his coffee and grimaced.

Apparently, we have the same opinion of coffee.

"Maybe you should talk with Peters. He is familiar with some of these symbols. Deals a lot with the occult criminal investigations."

Billy left the office to find Peters and gain some insight as to what, or to whom, the symbol might be connected.

Twenty-Six

"Hello?" Melody asked, unfamiliar with the number. She moved away from her chore of dishes, drying her hands on a kitchen towel.

"Hey, Melody—it's Mae." Her voice held an uncharacteristic tremble.

"Are you okay? You sound worried." Melody pulled out the chair at the table and took a seat.

"Yeah, no ... I mean, I'm okay, just need to talk. Do you think you could meet me at the deli on Fifth for a bite?" Her voice rose just a bit at the end.

"Sure, I can get there in fifteen minutes." Melody was already heading to the door, grabbing her purse as she finished the call.

"Great. I'll see you there." Mae hung up the phone.

Melody selected a booth in the back and ordered an iced tea for herself and a Diet Coke for Mae while she waited for her friend to arrive. The drinks had just come when Mae bustled through the door. She seemed to always have multiple bags in addition to her own bulk, which made navigating the small restaurant difficult. Bumping into chairs and accidentally hitting patrons in the head with her purse, Mae plowed her way down the aisle with numerous apologies. She looked frazzled.

Mae sat down with a huff, pulling bag, purse, and canvas tote across her ample bosom, nearly knocking over her drink. She dropped them into the space beside her in the booth.

"Melody." She gasped. "You won't believe what I just learned." Mae took a long drink of Diet Coke and paused.

She was not short of dramatic effects.

"Well, it's why I'm here. What I really want to know is why you sounded so worried. Now, spill the beans!" Melody took a slow drink of her tea.

"Well, Ethan … that's my new boss. Remember the job I told you about?" Mae asked.

"Yes. I see you took the position. Frank must be thrilled."

"Ha!" Mae burst. "So long as dinner isn't late, he's great!" She turned in her seat and looked around, surveying the room. Turning back to Melody, she leaned in conspiratorially.

"Ethan called me into his office today for a meeting. Nothing new there; he calls me in at least three times a day. Seems he can't write an idea down for himself. He wants to dictate everything. But that's fine. It's why I get paid." She took another drink of soda. "But the idea. Oh, my! What an overreach!" And just like that, the whisper was gone.

Melody cocked her head, lost in Mae's account.

Mae picked up on her expression, waving her hands as she spoke. "Well, yes, I need to start from the start. He called on the pager to come right away. Of course, I offered to bring him a snack from the break room. I needed tea anyway. He sounded irritated. I think he just hates happy people—"

"Generally, when your boss asks you to come in right away, he doesn't expect you to swing by the break room." Melody looked up as the waitress approached.

Mae ordered a meatball sub with extra sauce on the side, and Melody asked for an antipasto salad. The waitress collected their menus and rushed off to place the order.

Settling back into the conversation, Mae continued. "Well, that would explain the frustrated tone he took with me when I got there. He actually rolled his eyes at me!" Mae looked shocked. "But it was just a moment, and I was there, sitting ready to take notes. I pulled the pencil from my bun and had my notepad ready."

"Ummm ... does he not supply you with a laptop?" Melody inquired.

"Well, yes, but they're so hard to use, dear. Cumbersome things, actually. There is nothing so reliable as a pencil and pad of paper!" Mae assured her with an emphatic head bob.

Melody struggled against a smile. "Okay, so pencil in hand ...," she prompted.

"Yes, yes." Mae drew her hand under her chin and tapped the side of her cheek with a finger. "Right, so I settled into the chair across from his desk. Uncomfortable things, I sink so far back and they're irritatingly low to the ground. I had to put my tea on his desk—and you should've seen the look he gave me then!" She guffawed, drawing the attention of a few guests that her purse had assaulted on her way in. "It left a ring right on the glass top." She snickered. "Anyhoo, as soon as I sat down, the Holy Spirit push came over me. I started praying for him right there! Not out loud, of course, just in my mind. But if all those years on the mission fields taught me anything, it was to be obedient to the Spirit's instructions."

"Like in our Bible study ... doing what God asks when He asks so we don't lose the blessing," Melody chimed in.

"Yes, dear, exactly that!" She slapped the table, shaking the drinks.

The waitress stopped over to let them know the order had been placed.

"Could you be so kind as to get me a refill?" Mae asked brightly. "I love to have a backup at the ready. Thank you!

"Well"—she jumped right back in as the waitress stepped away—"I nodded to let him know I was ready, and he started talking all about this newfangled idea he had. 'My new initiative is called Homeless Humanity,' he told me. Their goal is to enable society to see humanity in those around them who are lost, homeless, and without hope. Sounds good, right? But listen, Melody. He wants to *seek out* the homeless and provide them with shelter, food, clothing, education, and training—a job within their community and an opportunity to restore themselves within our society. He said he would *enlist the help of the authorities* to transport these people to the new *compounds and ensure they remain within the new facilities.*" Mae emphasized each word with a tap of her finger on the table.

Melody's mouth fell wide. "He used those exact words?"

Mae's head nodded so hard her bun almost fell out. "Sounds like a prison, right? That's what I told him." She jutted her chin forward, a stern expression on her face. "I looked him right in the eye, you see, and kept pressing him, 'Where are you going to place them? What if they don't want to go? What measures will you enforce to keep them there?' Melody, I am really concerned about the invasive nature of this idea. I can't be the only one who sees where this concept could go!" Her brow was furrowed, and a frown pulled at the corners of her mouth.

Melody stabbed at the meat on her plate, "Who wouldn't be? How out of touch is this guy?"

"That's what I was thinking! You want to know what he said?" she asked, and it was Melody's turn to nod emphatically. "'Who wouldn't want a place to live? Housing is a human right!' Oh geesh, I had to look away so he wouldn't see me roll my eyes." She examined the meatball sub, spread out and taking up her entire plate, and opted for the knife and a fork. Cutting it up, she continued bringing Melody up to speed.

"I pressed him, 'But what if they don't want to go where you tell them to go?'" She pushed in a bite of the meat, sauce, and bread and continued speaking. "'The facilities will be new,' he tells me. 'Every person will have their own room. Families will be able to stay together in small housing units. They will learn new skills, and eventually, the goal is to restore them to our society.' He was obviously impressed by his own ideas.

"But I said, 'How do you know that they're family? Besides, it may be a fine idea to offer, but people *like* their freedom. They *like* to come and go as they please.' I don't know … it seems to be a slippery slope, to me. But what do I know? I'm just the secretary." She took a gulp of the soda and looked at Melody.

"What did he say? Did he consider your objections?" Melody was leaning forward, elbows on the table, iced tea in hand.

"Nope. He just moved on. Started talking about the tax write-off for businesses that wanted to support it and how he could send these 'reconstructed' homeless people to work there in return. Something about low-cost labor force. I had plenty more objections, but aside from some facial expressions—" She grimaced. "I just wrote down the notes."

Mae took another bite, held her finger up as she swallowed it down with some more soda, and continued. "This was the icing on the cake, my friend. This is what I really wanted to tell you—it's funded by Draven Wolfe."

Melody set her iced tea down a little too hard, trying to swallow it without choking. The drink splashed onto her plate and onto the table. Mae immediately reacted and grabbed napkins to mop up the spill. "That is exactly what I did!"

Melody processed all of Mae's story but focused on this last bit of information: Draven Wolfe. A billionaire with his slimy fingers sunk into countless areas across the country. Rumor mills churned with ideas of the things he supported. Anything that might push an evil agenda, turning families against one another, deepening divisions in society, and sowing discord wherever he could. Why would he be interested in Ethan's proposal?

Her spirit quickened, and she knew they would need to double down in their prayers that week.

Twenty-Seven

Billy had just reached his desk when he noticed Chief Stone was meeting with some men in his glass-enclosed office. His look was grim.

Billy watched the men as the conversation continued. He placed his briefcase and phone on the desk without taking his eyes off the three men. Soon, the chief rolled his desk chair back and pulled himself to his full height of six feet five inches. He walked to the window and waved Billy in. It was a command, not an invitation. Billy knew—it was the Feds.

This should be interesting, he thought wryly, grabbing his phone off the desk and heading for the office.

"Where's Dixon?" the chief asked as Billy entered. The room was clean, minimal. He had some awards on the wall, a family photo on his desk, and a couple of chairs. A large file cabinet fit under the window that the chief was standing at moments before. It provided a clear view of the lines of desks of his officers.

"Called off sick, I guess." Billy shrugged as he leaned against the file cabinet, stretching his legs in front of him and resting one ankle on the other.

"This is Agent Paul Wright and Agent Amir Malik, from the Bureau."

Chief Stone returned to his desk and took a seat. The Feds were already sitting in the two chairs on the opposite side of his desk.

Billy assessed the men as the chief spoke. Wright was clean cut, but soft in the middle. *Too many easy nights.* Malik seemed sharp. While Billy observed from the sidelines, Malik shifted his focus from Chief Stone to Billy.

Billy turned his attention back to Stone, who came to the point. "They have an interest in the missing-child case you've been working." He leaned back in his chair as if to say he had done his part, bringing all parties up to speed and it was up to them to hash it out the rest of the way.

Wright began. "Lily Chamberlain is a high-profile case for us. Her father has been with the Bureau for fifteen years. We know you received a tip about shipping containers, and we wanted to know if you have made any progress in the case beyond that."

Billy was only semi-stunned. He knew the case had been followed as he had been working closely with the parents. "Unless I start knocking on every shipping crate in the county, I'm not sure what good that tip was. The gentleman who left it supplied no contact information. And we have no more fresh leads." He shook his head in frustration yet again, with a slight hope that these men might have something they were willing to share.

"That gentleman was James Walker." Malik spoke this time. He had been sitting silently, as his partner drove the conversation. He leaned slightly forward. "He and his brother have run high-end escort services in this area for the last five years. More Ethan than James. You may have noticed his limp?"

Billy nodded, remembering it clearly.

"Yes." Malik continued. "Up until that moment, we never saw James act apart from Ethan. Not because they agreed on things, but because James is a bit slow and never challenged his brother. It's a very interesting turn of events." Malik silently held Billy's stare a bit longer.

"How do you know this?" Billy shifted his weight to both feet.

"We have a guy undercover. Working as one of Ethan's closest bodyguards. He's been on the job for almost seven months. He knows how it works.

"We have an idea we would like to propose," Wright said. "It's risky for both parties involved. We see there may be a break in the business. If James is willing to sell out his brother, we may have a chance to get in and obtain some hard evidence. If he's got Lily, then he's trafficking minors. Thing is, that wasn't his MO until recently. In order to see what has changed, we suggest that one of you go undercover as a client. You or your partner. We can get you to the right location. You would have to infiltrate and convince one of the girls to talk."

Billy balked at the thought. "You know how these victims are! It's Stockholm syndrome times ten. They've been abused mentally and physically by the same people who are providing their food and shelter. Sometimes for years! If it's not fear that keeps them there, it's loyalty. Just what do you expect us to find?"

Wright began to argue, but Malik cut him off with a simple raised hand, not moving from his position in the chair. "It's simple, officer. We expect you to find women, maybe children, who are being held against their will, perhaps even forced into sexual slavery. We have reason to believe this is part of a larger ring that is being overseen by Draven Wolfe."

The name hung in the air between the two men.

"Draven Wolfe?" Billy stood to full height. "How? Why? He's a billionaire. Why would he be connected with this?"

Wright replied. "What reason outside of money and power?"

Billy mulled it over for a moment. "I'm in." His anger and hopeless frustration of the last two weeks took a slight dip as he realized there might finally be another lead. He was going to take it.

Twenty-Eight

Scott slammed the pan in the sink and stormed out the door without a kiss or even a goodbye. Melody couldn't believe the frustration in her husband's voice. She hadn't done anything out of the ordinary; not to say her ordinary wasn't filled with incidents. She did seem to attract chaos. But it didn't warrant such anger from him, and it was unlike him to leave without resolution.

She sat down at the table, hoping to pray. She was able to lay aside the argument about her instructing him on the best way to clean the pan and opened her notebook. Her sons burst into the kitchen, fighting and bickering.

"How could you leave me, man?" Andrew pushed his sleeves up his forearms. "I had to have Patrice take me home, and she's crazy!"

"Sorry, I was ready to leave, so I left. I told you I was going," Ben replied with a simple shrug, as though justified.

"Guys, what happened?" Melody massaged her neck. *I need more coffee.*

They both proceeded to tell her their sides of the story at the same time, each one trying to over talk the other. Having dealt with this process for many years, Melody was quite skilled at ferreting out the bones of the issue and walked them through a resolution. Satisfied, they left the room, and peace returned to the kitchen. Momentarily.

"Gosh, Mom, you're already sitting around?" Her daughter's cutting tone dripped with sarcasm. "We're not all out the door yet. You can pretend like you do stuff around here until we leave."

"This is warfare," Melody mumbled to herself as it dawned on her. "You can take that tone and those words out with you as you take the trash to the curb." She fished a pen out of her purse. "Thank you."

Even in her bad temper, Grace knew better than to challenge or disobey her mother. So, with a gruff and disgruntled protest, she took the trash out.

Melody pushed the chair back with a little too much force as she stood, slapped her notebook closed, and grabbed her Bible. The kitchen was apparently not going to work as a refuge to study today. She moved to her bedroom, where she finally had a moment to herself, and spent it in solitude, sitting peacefully in the wingback chair by the large window. She felt the Spirit as He began to move, filling her thoughts and mind with a new language and indescribable peace. She released the frustrations of the morning and enjoyed the sweet company.

The phone rang, pulling her from her time with Jesus. When she picked it up, Beth offered a bright hello.

"You just won't believe the week I've had." Melody spoke into her phone. After getting up from her place by the window, she walked to the kitchen to get the dog's leash. A good walk gave her and the dog the exercise they both needed. Cooper followed at her heels. "It's just been like the enemy has targeted us. My kids are angry, my husband's angry. I'm angry. And we are happy people! I know it's warfare, but this is as hard as it gets. I will not be deterred! I will continue to fight and find time to spend in prayer. I keep walking and praying and focusing on the cities and county. I just keep praying that hearts are changed, and lives are freed!" She secured the leash, grabbed her journal from the counter, and headed out the door.

"I know!" Beth agreed. "Us too. It just means we are over the target! Have you gotten any words? I had such a weird dream last night. I feel silly even telling you this one."

Melody caught the tinge of nerves in Beth's laugh.

"Please share it. I know what you mean. I feel the same way about the words, but I will just be obedient, and if it means something, the Lord will show it!" She felt her burdens of the day lifting, and her tone became light and breezy.

"Well, I was in my bathroom, and I saw a cockroach. I tried to kill it three times by slapping it with my shoe, but it just got up and ran away. But as it ran away, you know how dreams don't move logically? Well, it changed from a cockroach to a little fox. I have no idea what that could possibly mean!"

Melody took in a quick breath and let out a low whistle. "Well, my friend. I'm pretty sure it means something. Here are the words I've received this week."

She juggled the leash as she riffled through the pages in her journal.

"Okay, here it is. 'Distribution of the phenomenon.' I had been praying for God to clearly show me that all this was from Him. Then I got '—To Balak.' I don't know about that one."

"Wasn't Balak the king of the Moabites—the ones who believed in child sacrifice?" Beth interjected.

"What? Oh, I don't know. How do you know these things?" Melody pulled her golden retriever away from a trash can.

Beth laughed. "Yes, random bits of Bible knowledge get stuck in my brain like food in my teeth. I don't know where they come from and usually don't even know that they're there until someone points it out!"

"Child sacrifice though. Interesting. Well, then I got 'the Black.' 'To capsize or invert.'" Melody paused. "Now this next one, I find interesting considering your dream. 'To be used,' but it was followed by 'fox, cunning.'"

"What? You have to be kidding me!" Beth sounded like she was choking.

"Are you okay?" Melody asked.

"Yes, sorry. Wrong pipe."

"Seriously, though. What do you think it means?"

"Well—" Her voice was softer. "It's kind of dark ... I'm connecting Balak to child sacrifice. We see our world today; how dark and evil it can be ... What if we are dealing with some form of child sacrifice? Human trafficking keeps coming to mind for both of us. Maybe we should be praying for more than that. Think of the dream that I had, the girl in green. What if …"

"What if what?" Melody prodded when Beth paused.

"What if the girl is real, Melody? And God is using us in bigger ways than we think."

Melody was not caught off guard. "I've been having the same thoughts, Beth. Honestly, it is so overwhelming, but He is the same God for you and for me—speaking to us both in part so we can make the connections together." She paused, thinking through how to say what she wanted to say. Cooper objected, pulling against the leash, even as his tail wagged.

"He has done much more dramatic things than raise up two housewives to pray for people stuck in a dark place. He has parted seas, flooded the world; He allowed a donkey to speak. Why wouldn't He use us today? Until a few weeks ago, I thought the gifts of the Spirit were just for the Apostles. Now look at us!" She shook her head in wonder. "I think she may be real. And I think we are a part of her story. And even if she's not, there are so many caught up and dragged into the industry who are. We may be praying for a very real, very specific girl, but we are definitely praying for thousands stolen and subjected to the cruelty every day."

"I feel like even if we never meet her here, we will meet her in heaven," Beth said. "I don't think our prayers are what started this. I think it was hers."

"What do you mean?" A cat jumped across the path, and Cooper went crazy. Melody was momentarily distracted, trying to rein him back in.

"Well, I was just thinking of this the other day. What if God has chosen us for this battle, but it was based on her prayers for help?" Beth sounded a little timid. "I just don't think you wake up one day and start praying for victims of human trafficking, and here we are doing exactly that. Maybe we should have been praying against it all along, but we weren't. We were happy in our bubbles. No, we were awakened to this."

"Well." Melody processed the insight of her friend. "Even more reason to keep going, despite the enemy's attacks."

Twenty-Nine

"Mrs. Everett."

Standing at the counter checking in the girls for an appointment, Beth bristled as Dr. Clark touched her arm.

"Hello, Dr. Clark. I think there's been some confusion. We are here to see—"

"Dr. Morrison," Clark interrupted. "Yes, I know. I just wanted to say that I believe we got off on the wrong foot. I think you may have been mistaken."

Beth considered her words. She didn't believe for one minute that she had been mistaken, but it was possible that she had been too harsh, too rash. Even now as Dr. Clark spoke to her, she was looking at the girls—well, really at Esther. Maybe that was good for a pediatrician.

"Thank you for the kind words, Dr. Clark. I will consider them."

Bridget, the receptionist, awkwardly interrupted the conversation. Dr. Clark moved to the other counter but stood within listening range.

"I'm so sorry, Mrs. Everett. Dr. Morrison was called to the hospital today."

Maggie let out a whimper, and Esther tried to console her sister by rubbing her back. "Oh, that is unfortunate. Normally I would reschedule, but Maggie is complaining of a sore throat and stomach trouble …" She trailed off, considering her options.

"The other physicians are also booked. We tried to call you, but it was rather sudden. We are so sorry for the inconvenience."

"Bridget." Dr. Clark had moved back to check-in and was peering over her shoulder. "I'm sure I could fit Maggie in."

"Really?" Bridget smiled brightly. "That would be wonderful. Mrs. Everett, is that okay with you? I do see a note in your chart …"

A brief cloud shadowed Dr. Clark's face.

"Well …" Beth considered. Last-minute decisions were never her best. But it was Dr. Clark or urgent care. "I guess this one time."

"Very well then," Dr. Clark sang. "I'll see you in the exam room momentarily."

After she walked away, Beth made a point to tell Bridget to keep the note on the chart. She still had her misgivings.

In the exam room, Maggie lay on the table. She really wasn't feeling herself, and Beth was concerned. She was running a low-grade fever and had a wet cough along with her sore throat and stomachache. After waiting for nearly thirty minutes, Beth was starting to get frustrated. A nurse had been in to take vitals and document the symptoms more than twenty minutes before.

"Mommy, I want my bed," Maggie complained, and a cough followed.

Beth placed a hand on her daughter's brow. The fever seemed to be climbing.

I know she worked us in, but this is ridiculous. I'll just take Maggie to urgent care. She put her coat back on and was helping Esther with her pink puffer coat before stirring Maggie.

A quick knock on the door was followed by Dr. Clark's arrival and profuse apologies for making them wait.

"I am working you in, you understand. So I had to see some of the other patients. But here I am, and here you are. Oh? You're not leaving again, are you?" There was a thick sweetness in her words, but her expression was scornful.

"I was about to, actually." Beth bristled at her reprimand. "We have been waiting for quite some time, after all. I do appreciate you working her in, but if you were too busy to see her, you should have been forthright. I could have been in and out of the urgent care by now and had her home in bed."

"I see. Well, you are of course welcome to do that, but I am here now," the doctor stated but did not make a move toward the child or the computer.

The two women seemed to be in a battle of wills. Who would relent? Beth, hating confrontation, finally decided it was the right thing to do and began to remove her and Esther's coats.

"Very well." Dr. Clark clapped her hands lightly and sat down at the computer. "I see the nurse has made some notes, but would you tell me what is going on with Maggie?"

Irritated, Beth repeated the same story she had now shared with three other people in the office. The scheduler, the front desk receptionist, and the nurse.

"I see." Dr. Clark did a brief exam on Maggie, looking in ears and throat. "Say ah," she instructed.

Maggie obeyed. The child winced against the pain in her throat.

"It looks like it could be strep throat. I'll have the nurse take a swab and prescribe an antibiotic for her. Does she have any allergies?"

"No, none that I know of," Beth replied. "Thank you, Doctor." It took all of Beth's good nature to be civil.

"Well, when she gets to feeling better, maybe you could check out a park close to your address. It's a quaint little spot with a fun playground, a field, and nice benches for Mom." Dr. Clark sounded warm and friendly.

Beth nodded her head, faintly discomfited that Dr. Clark knew where they lived. She bundled up the girls and headed back home. She would have Billy stop and pick up the medication on his way home from work.

Thirty

Cassie jarred to attention, as the overhead fluorescents flooded the small space with sudden light. Ethan entered, fidgeting with his sleeve cuffs. He cracked his knuckles and looked around the room. She thought it odd that he would have any reason to be nervous.

James slid in behind him and skulked over to the right corner. He limped to a stop and tried to make eye contact with her.

Looking away, she touched her stomach instinctively, trying to hide the bump that was changing her profile. She knew she had to be through the first trimester. When they realized it, she knew what they would do. So far, Missy had kept her secret, but she didn't know how long that would last.

Draven entered a few moments after Ethan. As his tall frame filled the door, Cassie felt like the room somehow got colder.

"This is it, Draven. This is what you've asked for. I continue to build the supply." Ethan cleared his throat. "We have forty-seven spaces across this city alone." He offered a weak, sweeping gesture with his arm. Seemingly reduced to his boyish days, his air of authority vanished under the scrutiny of this man. "If you had given me more notice, I would have …" He trailed off at Draven's scathing glare.

Draven took three steps into the room, raising his nose as though he smelled something foul, and slowly surveyed each of the captives. The fluorescent lights had been on long enough for their eyes to adjust, and Cassie had a clear look at the man. The first time he came in, his stay was brief. She still remembered the girl.

Now she stole glances from the corner of her eye, not daring to make direct eye contact. He stood strong. Cassie imagined he controlled more than just Ethan.

He stared the longest at Missy. A slow smile of recognition split his face. Missy responded with a look of pure fear. Cassie heard her catch her breath. Observing the vivid reaction, Cassie watched Missy's eyes expand and her teeth begin to chatter.

"Missy" was all he said, and he turned and left the room.

Cassie watched as the new guards sprang into action. They came from the doorway to haul her away. Cassie felt compelled to cry out in protest, but when Tommy took her hand softly in his and their eyes met, she was silenced. The message was clear—if they took Cassie, or hurt her, or … killed her, who would be left to help them?

Missy showed no signs of struggle. She hung her head and, shoulders slumped, simply walked with them out the door. Cassie couldn't piece it all together; Missy had battled everyone every step of the way—until now. She was fire and fury, yet now she walked out as a wounded lamb.

Ethan came further into the room and selected Cassie and seven others. "You have a party tonight. Get showered and ready. We leave in an hour."

The children Ethan had chosen for tonight's event got busy getting ready. The shower was cold. James came in right on schedule with outfits for them. Apparently, they were to dress as little boys and girls for tonight's show.

He hung back as Cassie started to get dressed.

"I really wish you didn't have to go," he whined.

As if it's my choice, she fumed as she put on the blue and white jumper. She had neither the words nor the patience for his mind-numbing ignorance. Realizing he had been raised in this, and he had no concept of anything different, she just could not keep playing this game.

There seemed to be something else he wanted to tell her. She waited for him to speak. He slipped back into the quiet of his thoughts.

Trying a different tactic, Cassie asked a simple question. "James, do you know who Jesus is?" She didn't bother to look up as she pulled up the knee-high white stockings. Honestly, she didn't even believe he would hear or understand a word of the gospel.

"The dead guy on the necklace?" He spread his arms out in mockery with a half-smile on his face.

Ignoring his insults, she persisted. "Did you know he rose from the grave?" This time she did pause and held his gaze.

He awkwardly fumbled and looked away.

"The Bible you gave me—it was from your mom?"

He made himself really busy with his boots, avoiding any contact. "Ethan says that religious stuff is weak and fairy tales. He used to pray …" He trailed off, seemingly uncomfortable with the topic.

For the first time, Cassie saw James as a person instead of her captor. Refusing to fall prey to foolish notions that he was good, just for a moment she saw the little boy that was beaten and bruised by a world that had no place for him and even less compassion. Her heart softened.

"Well, He is not a fairy tale, James. He came here to die for us, all of us. Me. You. Your brother. He sacrificed Himself so we could live with Him forever. It's simple really."

Cassie paused, touching his hand as he looked her in the eye for the first time since the conversation began.

"And it's true. James, eternity is forever. It will be forever in Heaven or hell. I've had enough of hell right here, haven't you?"

He had to cough all of a sudden and turned away. She knew she had been obedient to God.

"I went to the cops," he said, barely above a whisper. He turned from her, rubbing his hands up and down his pant legs.

"What?" Astonishment banished all other words from her mind. She looked over at Lily and Anna. Their eyes were round as they listened. *Thank God Missy isn't here right now.*

He turned back around and grabbed her by the shoulders. "Cassie, I know it isn't right. I know what is happening isn't right. It's not what Ethan wanted ... not the kids. That was the mean lady's idea. It's the only life we know. We came from this, you understand?"

He was in a battle in his mind. She saw the turmoil as it raged within him. He dropped his hands and began to pace.

"I didn't tell them anything. I just gave a sort of a clue is all. It's up to them to figure it out." He turned to face her with tears in his eyes. "We never meant for all of this—"

"James!" Melvin yelled. "Ethan is looking for you. Get your scrawny self out of here and stop harassing the girls. Go on now!"

Cassie felt panic rise—had Melvin and Amber heard any of his confession? Surely they saw his odd behavior. They treated him like he was a dog. And in many ways, he was. Just now, he seemed to tuck his tail and run from the room. But seeds were planted.

If she was destined to be bound to the man, she considered praying for him. Bile burned in her throat, but she prayed anyway. "Lord, as repulsive as he is to me, he is still Your child. Caught up in a world that is not of his choosing, he is simple, stupid really, and doesn't understand. Make Your truth clear to him, Father. Let him see You and know the sacrifice You made for him. And please let his clue make it to the right people." *Maybe ... just maybe.* She was too afraid to hope and banished the soft glimmer before it could take root. She had to fight to survive here, and fantasies had no place. If God was moving, she needed to see the evidence, not just could-be's.

She finished tying the blue bow in her blond hair and waited for the evening job to begin.

The routine was always the same. If you weren't selected for the job, you were to sit in the back of the room and face the wall. If you were selected, you were to sit on your knees, with your head bowed, hands in your lap, ready to be blindfolded. Most of the time, they left the kids' hands free, but only after they had proven themselves obedient.

The guards walked on either side of the children who would work the event. Two walked in front, binding their hands, tying the blindfolds. Two walked behind, knocking heads forward if they were too slow, smacking them if they showed any signs of disobedience.

"Cassie." Melvin sneered.

She extended her hands obediently yet felt the smack from behind anyway. *Amber.*

"You wanna say something, darlin'?" He teased as he bound her hands. Tightly.

She still had more to prove. They enjoyed the challenge. But was a sixteen-year-old girl really a challenge? To these sorry excuses for humans, apparently, yes.

The cold night air bit at her exposed thighs as she exited the rectangle room. The high-heeled Mary Jane shoes were a size too big, and Cassie stumbled against the guard. He righted her and smacked her backside hard, because he could. She held back a curse, knowing it would get more of the same attention. They had mocked her before.

Entering another van, she listened carefully to determine if they would all be in one vehicle. It seemed that way. It must have been a full-size van, or maybe a small bus since there were eight of them, plus the guards. She was just glad there were seats this time.

Pulling out of the parking lot, she felt the right turn and began to count the stops and turns as she had learned to do. Not sure why. Hope, maybe. *He went to the police.* She couldn't shake the hope from her heart. Twenty-eight, twenty-nine, thirty—another right turn. Anger boiled in her as she listened to the guards taunt and tease the boys in the back seat. If she only had a knife, what she wouldn't do.

Seventy-eight, seventy-nine ... she didn't count by minutes. She would lose track of how many had passed. Counting and then dividing by sixty seemed to be effective and she remembered one number more easily. So far, she had learned they were about seven minutes from a highway. She felt the short jaunt of the on-ramp, the rushing sound of semitrucks, and the increased speed of the vehicle. They were just merging now; an angry driver blasted his horn as the guard driving roared in laughter and expletives. If only that person knew what the van was hauling. Cassie always prayed for a car accident. They were never buckled up; surely, they would have injuries—but the alternative was ever so much worse. Even now, her stomach began to churn and tighten.

The van began to slow, and she recognized the off-ramp merge. The venues were always within minutes of the highway. They were close now.

Thirty-One

Billy felt calm before a storm. He had been brought up to speed regarding the Walker brothers. Ethan had fled an assault when he was ten. He disappeared for five years on the streets of Chicago, only to return to his hometown and exact revenge on the man who had beaten him and destroyed his brother. From there, he took James with him, and they fell into prostitution to pay off debts that Ethan had accrued.

That turned into drug running, and they eventually became dealers. About six months ago, Draven Wolfe had begun contracting with Ethan. Instead of running drugs, they had turned to running kids. The Feds, who had planted a mole a year ago, had enough information to bring them in, but they wanted the bigger prize. Draven's funding had lifted them from obscure mules to big-time dealers. They were now respected and wealthy, everything Ethan had ever wanted. James, as always, just followed his brother; he had nowhere else to go.

While sitting in the unmarked van in the alley, Billy reviewed the details for tonight's mission. He would have two minutes to spend with the girl before his team could interrupt the video surveillance. Once that was accomplished, he would have to move fast—provided he played the role well and didn't give these guys any reason to suspect him.

Twenty minutes later, Billy pretended to relax in a club chair, an untouched vodka and tonic on the small table to his right. Soon children would be joining them. He winced inwardly. His mission tonight was to determine whether there was a possible connection to make—a child who would be willing to talk.

He took in the scene around him and forced his fist to relax as the men and women in the room shared their excitement for the evening. He took note of each person in attendance. He recognized the two politicians from current county- and city-level campaigns. Their clean-cut suits and plastic smiles belied their true selves. Here in the dark, the ugliness of their souls was exposed.

To their left sat a man and two women. They had come as a group. The two women were young, maybe in their twenties. They could have been paid for as well, but Billy wasn't sure. Dripping in jewels and wearing tight-fitting, name-brand outfits suggested they had money or at least access to it. And next to Billy sat the other man. Slicked-back hair and a hunger in his eyes. Billy swore he could almost see a demon dancing in them.

He would interject in the conversation enough to sufficiently blend in. It took all he could give. The bartender was eyeing him suspiciously, so he joined a little more and the gaze relaxed. The atmosphere was electric, and soon, in addition to the alcohol, the drugs appeared, and white trails of powder transformed them into shells of the humans they were when they arrived. An animal intensity filled the place.

Billy's entire career could not have prepared him for what he felt when the eight children were led into the room. They were leashed, dressed as some sick kind of school children in white clothes, with royal-blue satin accents. The boys had white shorts with blue suspenders, and their chests were left bare. The girls were dressed in white jumpers with blue sashes and matching blue bows in their hair. They wore blue Mary Janes and white stockings to their knees.

He nearly vomited. The night would only get worse, yet he was bound to make no arrests tonight. An order that he wrestled with even more at this moment.

He immediately homed in on the tall blonde. The oldest by far, but there was still a fire in her eyes. She was willing to fight. Selections would be made quickly, and entertaining the idea of the younger ones would keep him above suspicion, before settling for the matron of the bunch. He could feel the bartender watching him again. As the new guy to the party, he really hadn't expected anything less.

Music raged. Alcohol flowed. And the drugs took their full effect on the crowd. Finally able to make the choice, he stepped up to the young woman and then followed her into the room that had been paid for and reserved.

The room was a small, tight space. One twin bed with questionable sheets haphazardly covering the mattress. A small bedside table held a small lamp and a clock blinking *12:00 AM*. The walls looked like they had the original wood paneling from 1974. The stench of old cigarettes and weed filled the air.

Billy relied on his team to hack into the video surveillance system and splice the bar's surveillance system to buy him several minutes of time to speak freely with the girl. Even now they sat in an alley nearby in an unmarked van. The hidden earpiece was his sole connection to knowing when they had succeeded.

He sat on the small twin with his feet on the floor, treating it like a couch. He reluctantly, yet convincingly, began his role.

Assuming the cameras were already watching, he directed her, buying time until his team disengaged the security feed. "Dance for me." He cringed.

She moved slowly to the small radio and turned on some soft music. The girl began to dance. Billy leaned over and raised the volume. "What's your name?" he asked, softly. He noted the time on his watch.

"Whatever you want it to be, baby." Her eyes closed.

"No, really. What is your name?" He insisted, trying not to push too hard and build suspicion. He had to see if she would be willing to disclose the truth of who she was.

"You can call me Cassie." Her eyes flew open, and he saw her flinch. Her expression revealed that she was speaking the truth. "Or Samantha, or Roxanne." She controlled her expression and fell back into the role he was paying for. "What you want, baby?" she asked sweetly.

"More than you can give." Relieved it didn't take long for her to share her name, but still waiting for confirmation that the feed was cut, he continued to play a part. He had to balance this with perfect timing.

"Course I can give you what you want. It's my job to make you happy," she purred.

The earpiece crackled. "It's a go, Billy."

He had to make the time count. Holding tight to caution, he had to determine what would assure this girl that he could be trusted.

"What would you do if I told you I could help you?" he asked in a hushed tone.

Her gaze faltered. He took her hand and pulled her to the bed, not allowing his body to touch hers, yet close enough to whisper in her ear.

"I can help you. Can I trust you?"

She took a short breath in, her eyes faltered before falling back under the hard veil. He knew he was losing her. He knew about the cameras; he knew what the punishment would be if the owner knew she was talking. The risk was more in her court than his. He hoped he had not wasted the night on the wrong kid.

"Ha!" Her voice was thick with emotion. She tried to blow him off, to keep playing the game, but he saw the tremble in her hand. "How can I know who to trust these days?"

He held her gaze. "You can trust me. My name is Billy Everett, I'm a cop."

"Is this the game?" Her face hardened. Putting her hands out in front of her, she returned to her role. "You want to cuff me, officer?"

She waited. He did not move. Her hands fell to her lap. "I'm Cassie Woods." She suddenly stood to pace the room. Her hands were balls of energy at her sides. "You know they record these rooms, right? If you get out of here alive, that's great for you. But once they review it, I'm dead. What do you want from me?" Her fear masqueraded as anger.

"Relax, Cassie," Billy commanded in a voice that calmed her. "That is your real name, yes?"

She nodded.

"You and I have about ten minutes before they come knocking on that door and my time is up. We have been tracking Ethan and his brother. They are now connected with Draven Wolfe. What we don't know is how or to what extent."

She sucked in a mouthful of air that made her cough hard. She sat back down on the bed.

"What can I do?" Once the fit subsided, her eyes were wet, not just from coughing. Slowly, she turned her face toward him, her eyes wide. "You can take me with you? I can go back home?" A single tear raced down her cheek.

Billy began to explain, but she interrupted herself.

"The others ..." She shook her head, lowered her gaze. "How could I leave them alone? They're just kids." She choked, the words barely more than a whisper. When she looked up at Billy through her tears, he almost decided to grab her and get out. But they needed to know how to find the network.

"How many kids are there?" He cupped her face in his hands with the tenderness of a father. "We need to know his locations. Can you tell me that?"

She shook her head slowly. "No, I don't know ... I mean there are like thirty of us where I am, but I heard them talk about more locations. I ... I don't even know what state I'm in. But I saw some streets one night ... the first time ..." Her voice was shaky, and she looked away from Billy and repeated what felt like a mantra she had memorized. "Church. Woodland. Sixty-sixth Avenue. Panda's Pizza. Rite Now Drugs.

"I know we are kept in a shipping crate." She seemed to be regaining her focus. "You know, like the ones on construction sites or on the big boats. But they must have done some alterations because there is a shower and a Porta Potty. They remove it once a week, but I think on random days."

She stood again, animated, "And I know Draven. He comes every so often to the rectangle room. At least two, maybe three times. And some fat lady. Nasty woman. She acts like she's in charge."

Billy was pleased. She was smart and she noticed key details. He stood as he made mental notes even as the information was being wired to the van outside. He noticed how her hand curled around her middle. Protecting ... the truth hit him like a truck. She was pregnant.

She was still spilling information. "I have all the details in my Bible." She looked at Billy. "He gave me a Bible and a pen. I write it all down and hide it in the corner." She returned to pacing. "It's small and the guards never check. They're so stupid. We are about seven minutes from a highway. We are kept in darkness, and it is so cold." Her body shivered and she rubbed her arms as if thinking about that. "I'm the oldest, and the youngest is Lily, and she's only seven." She looked at him again; he saw the plea in her eyes. "One girl told us that she saw the outside once, when they brought her in." She paused. "The container is blue, and it has 'W-B-I-U' on the outside of the door. And the snake in a circle—like it's eating its own tail. I think it's the same as some clients' tattoos. Those are all the details I remember."

In a wave, Billy saw despair overtake her. Her body slumped, her eyes faltered, and her voice wavered. "What can you do? What can I do? It's all hopeless. Ethan will not be found out. And Draven would kill us all first." She turned from him and placed her forehead in her hand, elbows rested on her lap. Her body shuddered with soft sobs.

Billy took her by the shoulders, forcing her to look at him. "Lily?" he said firmly. "You said she's seven? What color is her hair?"

"Why does it even matter?" She lamented. "Blond hair with blue eyes. There are so many little kids there. I know the risks here, I know they'll beat me just for crying and ... but ... someone on the outside has to know."

He still hadn't let go of her shoulders but was processing the information in his mind. "Lily is there, with you?" His tone was thoughtful as he processed the information. But he knew their time was limited, and filed the thought in his mind along with several other things that she had shared that were noteworthy. "Cassie," he commanded. "We are going to meet again. There is a plan forming for you and the others. And your child."

She gasped; her eyes widened. "How?"

"You cannot tell anyone we spoke, and you must act like everything is normal. Do you understand me?" He was pulling out his wallet. He took a small card from it and handed it to her.

She nodded shakily, taking the card.

"Listen to me. Focus! This is my number. Hide it—just in case you get a chance to call. There will be a distraction soon. You stay here. We will be in touch."

As he finished speaking, the sound of sirens pierced the air.

"Tell my mom I'm okay. Please. Tell her I love her!" she whispered. But he was already heading out the door. She tucked the card into her shirt.

Billy pulled the fire alarm by the back door as he escaped into the night, skirting the dumpster that nearly blocked the door.

Moments later, Cassie jumped when Ethan burst into the room. He took in the tear stains and the music; she was fully clothed. She thought he must have passed Billy on the way to the room.

"Get up!" he screamed. "We've got to go now!" He took a second glance as he was leaving the room and cursed. "What did you do?" Growling from deep in his throat, he ground out, "Never mind. Get going. Someone called us in."

Worried more about his own escape, he left without waiting for her. She followed at his heels. At the back door, heading into the alley, he collided with a dumpster. He cursed loudly and Cassie saw the jagged corner that broke through his jacket and shirt and slashed into his skin.

He turned back to her, holding his shoulder. "Wait for the guards."

Cassie stood at the open door, trembling and afraid. There was no time to process the night, and confusion filled the air. The sirens were closer now. She watched as the taillights of Ethan's SUV disappeared around the corner. Suddenly, Melvin and Hector were behind her, pushing the other children toward the door. She huddled them around her, guiding them through the dark and cold toward the van.

The guards didn't bother with blindfolds. Still prisoners, they were forced by the guards into the van. She felt thankful for the ability to help the kids in their panic. With guards rushing and pushing them into the waiting vehicle, Anna and Tommy fell into each other in the chaos. They were all crying. Cassie did her best to help them climb in.

The last guard landed hard in his seat, yelling to Amber to go as he shut the door. Reaching out to comfort the kids as the van careened down the dark alley, Cassie nestled them together in the dark.

Hector's voice boomed as he spat out commands. "Lie down! Close your eyes! Don't say a word!"

"Slow down, you idiot!" Melvin protested from the back seat. "You'll get us pulled over driving like this. Calm down!"

"Just shut those kids up, Melvin, and leave the driving to me!" Amber spat back.

Cassie thought about the night. She must have been insane to trust this guy. *But I do.* Considering his promises, and how he had cupped her face, brought her dad to mind. *You promised to protect me, Daddy. But here I am. You couldn't protect me. But I am the one who left.*

In the darkness of the van, with only a streetlamp lighting the interior every three seconds, the tears welled up and fell down her cheeks. The emotion was overwhelming.

Thirty-Two

Beth had made sure everything was ready for the Bible study today. It was the first time she was hosting, and she was both nervous and excited. Mae was unable to join the girls due to her new job, but Beth and Melody fell into easy conversation. Melody shared some new words she had received and some interesting things that had piqued her curiosity.

"I've received a series of words that I believe mean something. Tell me what you think, Beth. She-bear, helmet, walking, march, stuck, control, hump, and enveloped. They seem random, but so specific that I think they must have intentional purpose."

Beth paused. She had written the words down in her journal as Melody sounded them off. She mulled over each word, praying for the Spirit to provide clarity. "Hmmm." She spoke mostly to herself as she prayed softly. "She-bear … I feel like we are the she-bears. We are fighting fiercely and interceding for the kids that we know are forced—and presumably stuck—in this horrible industry. I think about the girl in green from my dreams. Even if she specifically does not exist, she represents the kids that do. Like the kids in Billy's case."

"Helmet makes me think of the armor of God." Melody offered.

"I agree. I think we are being called to put on the full armor and march. We are truly fighting this battle."

"We may be the only mamas praying for these kids." Melody pondered. "I mean, there are so many kids who go missing every year. Kids from every kind of home. Even though we want to believe it only happens to families in crisis, it isn't just them. Kids run away, they're stolen, they slip through the cracks of state-run foster care. There is no way to know just how many have been lost. Or how many have been sold."

The heaviness of the situation lay on the two women like a weight. Beth continued to consider the other words.

"So we know the kids are stuck, under someone else's control. But I think the words could have double meaning. I mean, God is ultimately in control, and if we stick to the prayer cover, He will hear our cry and move on behalf of those in need, right? As she-bears, we can move the mountain through our prayers. But hump? Hmmm. Hump day." She laughed.

"Maybe something has been put in motion and we are halfway through?" Beth continued speculating. "Enveloped … it could be as simple as we are surrounding her with our prayers. I don't know, Melody."

Beth looked up from the journal. "But it does seem that this is a push from God. An urge to pray for children in our country for protection and freedom. I mean, we hear the news about kids crossing the border, and we have no way to sort out whether they're coming with a brother or a handler. I read that more than sixty thousand kids have gone missing from foster care in less than twenty years. There are broken systems and a government full of angry, mudslinging blame casters. It doesn't seem like they can pull themselves together to unite for any cause. It's frustrating. But it's also not right for us to sit back and just complain. The government can't fix everything. But I know we serve a God who can bring unity and solutions. We just need to keep praying for these victims."

She leaned back in her chair, massaging her neck where the tension of the last few days had settled in knots.

"There is more." Melody shifted in her chair. She picked up the journal and placed it in her bag. "Do you know that old theater on Main Street? I pass it each week on my way to the laundromat. It's been closed for a few years now. I've noticed some strange activity. It may be nothing, but it strikes me as odd."

She took a sip of her coffee before continuing. "Two weeks ago, I noticed a bus parked there. The sunscreen was up in the front window as though the driver was sleeping there. I drove around back and found a moving truck. And there are storage containers back there."

Beth leveled her gaze at her friend. "Is your husband aware that you've been staking out this place?"

Melody offered a sheepish grin. "Well, not exactly. But listen. The day before yesterday, there were nine mattresses thrown out by the side of the property. Nasty mattresses. Old and stained. I'm pretty sure with blood, Beth. But when I happened to drive by on my way here … they were all gone."

"That is strange." Beth nodded.

"Well, I will drive by it later today when I go to do laundry. I'll just take a quick drive around. If there is anything suspicious, you can tell Billy to go look."

"Oh, yeah. That sounds good." Beth agreed. "But don't get out of your vehicle, okay?"

"Right." Melody said, but Beth was not convinced.

They sat for a few moments staring at their coffees.

Beth stood and reached for her purse. "Let's go."

Grabbing the keys, Melody matched her energy. Then they were out the door, heading to the movie theater.

Thirty-Three

Melody offered to drive, since she knew the precise location. Beth climbed into the black SUV and buckled. She couldn't take her mind off the images that flooded her. She rubbed her forehead, feeling a headache coming on. She wasn't sure how much more stress she could take.

Was the Lord revealing actual events or was her imagination running wild? She screamed a prayer in her mind for God to capture every thought and help her to maintain focus and to please, protect the children!

Melody drove with purpose. She weaved in and out of traffic and ran through about three yellow lights. She slowed down only as the theater came into view.

"Here we are." Melody's words hung ominously in the air.

Melody took a slow turn, and they crept through the parking lot, paying close attention to their surroundings. Beth took in every detail to record in the notebook she had pulled out of her purse. She had to flip through several pages of the girls' artwork to find a blank page.

It was a small theater. One of the main reasons it had been closed was the massive new cineplex that went in a few years ago, just a few blocks away.

Melody drove slowly by the front of the building. Beth noted the front doors.

"Look at the lock on the door. It's broken." She pointed with her pen and then jotted the detail down in her book.

The cement parking lot showed signs of being unkempt for years. Grass tufts fought their way through cracks, making them broader. Spray paint decorated the sides of the building from local kids making their presence known. Litter blew across the lot as they drove around to the back.

The three large shipping containers in the back of the lot would make sense if there had been any construction. Situated against the back fence and a large dumpster, the containers took up much of the back lot.

Melody drove the route between the theater and the containers. Beth noted a small detail on the middle container. It appeared to be a snake in a circle. She made a full loop and parked the truck just before the dumpster.

"Dang it. The mattresses are gone." She smacked the steering wheel before pointing to where they had been. "I should've guessed ... Well, this is where they were last week. Right next to the dumpster. Like I said, I counted nine of them. There were so many stains on them. Seriously, Beth, why on earth would there be mattresses at an abandoned movie theater? I thought maybe it was the homeless, but even if it was them, they wouldn't throw them away. And there are no other signs of people. No trash bags or shopping carts. Nothing."

Beth shook her head in bewilderment. Her hand found its way to the door handle.

"Now, hold on, Beth," Melody cautioned her. "You're the one who warned me not to get out of the vehicle! We should stay in the truck. I don't know if there is anyone here. Or dogs, or ..."

But, with an apologetic smile and shrug of her shoulders, Beth slipped out of the vehicle and headed toward where Melody had just pointed.

She looked back just long enough to watch Melody throw open the door and join her in the search for clues. Or evidence.

Beth walked slowly around the small area between the back lot and the trees beyond the property. Her breath came in puffs as it hit the cold air. She pulled her coat tighter, attempting to chase the chill from her heart. It wasn't unusual to have a late blast of winter, but she hadn't planned on being outside this long. Snow had sprinkled the ground, leaving patches of white in the dead grass. She could identify rabbit tracks in some of the more covered spots. Odd to think how time and life passed by while such evil existed in the world. As her eyes followed the rabbit trail, she saw narrow black strips jutting out of the weeds.

She took a few steps and from a short distance realized what they were, and her heart fell. Zip ties. Still secured on one end, the loop had been cut. She couldn't keep the tears from her eyes.

In an instant, she heard a man yelling, a dog growling, and Melody shouting.

"Beth! We have to go! Now!"

Beth whipped around and took in the scene, frozen. A stocky man was shouting at them in broken English, his accent thick. Barely controlled, and headed straight for her, the pit bull was frantically barking. She bolted for Melody who had already made it into her SUV. She slowed, looking back at the objects on the ground. To turn around now would be insane, taking her further from the safety of the SUV and closer to the growling dog already closing the gap. The large animal slipped and yelped.

Beth seized the opportunity and with a prayer for protection ran for the objects. She grabbed what she could as the man screamed at her in a foreign language and released the dog. She turned and bolted for the truck. Breathing heavily and gasping for air, more from panic than exertion, she dove into the passenger side door that Melody had opened for her. The ferocious animal lunged toward her. The door slammed shut as the dog bared its teeth. Its paws scraped the glass, and it barked loudly at the window.

Melody threw the car in gear and peeled out. Beth looked back to see the man talking on his phone.

Inside the truck, Melody was half crying, half laughing—caught between terror and exhilaration. She mumbled to herself about this madness. They both became quiet and lost in their thoughts as they replayed the incident in their minds. That it all just happened in broad daylight was mind-boggling.

"Oh my gosh. Beth! Did that just happen?" Melody exclaimed, breaking the silence, as she pulled them into the safety of a grocery store parking lot.

Beth was still trembling. She held the items in her lap, mixed with bits of dry grass and dirt. The melted snow left splotches of mud on her jeans. Her fingernails had dirt caked inside, and two were broken. She had jammed one finger into the frozen ground as she grabbed the items, and it was starting to swell.

She looked over at her friend in a daze. "I can't believe I just did that. I have never in my entire life …" She trailed off, shaking her head. "Melody, this was never just a dream."

Both ladies looked at the evidence Beth had collected. Beth had managed to grab three of the zip ties. She was startled to find she also had a simple gold ring mixed in with the items.

They looked at the items, then at each other, still feeling the surreal awe of the situation. Beth examined the ring in her hand, and discovered it was engraved with a Bible verse. "We need to get this to Billy."

Melody already had the SUV in gear and was backing out.

Thirty-four

Melody loaded the last of the towels from the washing machine into the dryer. She had spent entirely too much time scoping out the movie theater with Beth. Now the day had slipped away, and she was finishing her chore in the dark. She had finished three loads already. After the dryer was humming, she picked up the basket full of clothing and walked to the door. Using her back to open the door, she nearly stumbled as a young man pulled the door open—the same man-child who seemed to be there every time she was. *Does he watch for me?* Maybe he was trying to be courteous, but the smile on his face was menacing. She smiled, mumbled a thank-you, and pressed by him toward her SUV.

She placed the basket in the back with the other two and climbed into the front seat. She started the vehicle, turned on the heat, put her cell phone on the charger, and pulled out a novel to pass the time. Fifteen minutes went by, then twenty.

"Well, it could be dry by now. I'll go check." Announcing the plan to herself, she was nervous, though she didn't know why. This had been her routine for months now, and that young man had been hanging around just as long. She shook her head, steadied her hand, and chased the fear away. She turned off the SUV, grabbed her purse and headed for the building. Halfway there, she realized she had forgotten her phone. *It's okay. I'm just grabbing the last two loads. I'll fold them at home.*

It was already getting dark; the lights in the parking lot flickered. The dull yellow of the fluorescents indicated they needed replacing. She hustled across the lot to the door and entered the laundromat with two other men.

The men met up with the kid, fist bumps, side hugs … *Did that man just slip something to the other guy?* Her pace slowed as she assessed the new visitors. The young man had always made her edgy, but the other two filled her with apprehension. One of the new strangers had sandy blond hair and wore low riding pants with a baggy dark plaid button-down shirt over a dirty undershirt. The other had a tattoo of a snake and a star over his right eye. He chuckled as she walked by, and his friend let out a low whistle. She nearly jumped when the buzzer sounded on the dryer.

She moved quickly toward the dryer which held her clothing. Reaching into her bag, she cursed herself for leaving her phone in the truck. She unloaded the clothes, struggling to grab a wayward sock. Eager to be out the door and safely in her car, she didn't bother folding any of the items. Heading directly for the door, she tried not to let the panic overtake her when the men moved into her path.

"Hey, pretty lady," the friend started. When he winked at her, the snake tattoo seemed to slither. His black mohawk merged into his neck tattoos.

"I just am looking to head home, guys. Please let me pass." She tried to sound firm, though her voice trembled.

"No worries. No worries." Tattoo man assured her, raising his hands innocently, yet moving menacingly around her. "Our friend tells us you come here every week. He told us you were so pretty. We just wanted to see for ourselves."

"Really. Thanks. I … um … I really need to leave." *Where is the employee? He's never around when I need him. Probably in the back sleeping.*

They surrounded her.

She was in a full-blown panic now, trying to remember every trick she ever learned for a situation like this. A situation she never really expected to be in.

"You don't have to be in a hurry," the young man taunted. "You should be nice to my friends."

She slapped his hand away as he tried to touch her hair.

He frowned. "You tease me every week, and now you want to be nasty?"

Her mouth fell open in surprise. She knew she was in trouble.

They moved simultaneously. Mohawk knocked the laundry basket out of her hands. The man in the dirty shirt grabbed her by the hair, while the kid snatched her purse and ran from the room. She cried out as her head was yanked back, the man's face so close she could see the meat stuck in his teeth, the heat of his breath across her cheek. With a quick move, he smacked her across the face, warning her against calling out for help. His friend laughed like a madman, standing guard by the door.

"Hurry up, man," he cackled. "I want a turn."

Tattoo began to work his belt buckle. Probably mistaking her stillness for obedience, he let go of her hair, and Melody moved into action. She brought her knee up hard and fast, causing him to double over in pain. Mohawk was quick, moving in with a punch across her face. She fell to the ground, and they began to kick her. The door jingled again. Assuming it was the kid, she was confused when they both cursed and ran out of the room. Still, she was too scared to look up. She dragged in a deep, ragged breath, trying to stave off the panic attack. Blood trickled down her face, underneath her hair. Her ribs screamed.

After a few moments of silence and no more abuse, she tentatively peered out through strands of hair to see a very large, dark-skinned man standing by the door. "You are safe now," he assured her. His accent was thick.

He held out her purse and helped her pick up the laundry. She watched him, not quite ready to move from her place on the floor. *He must be almost seven feet tall. Where on earth did he come from?*

"Th ... thank you," she stammered, in shock from the attack. He placed a careful arm around her and helped her stand.

He ducked to get through the door, then walked her to her car and waited while she got in. Trembling, she locked the doors, looked in the mirror, and began to cry. Her entire body was shaking. Who was that man? She looked back to take one more look, but the parking lot was empty once again.

I think I just met my angel.

Thirty-five

Beth sat on the weather-worn bench, warming herself in the fading afternoon sunlight. They had caught a beautiful day in mid-May, although with a slight chill. This was their new favorite park, and she managed to get the girls there once or twice a week, even during the rainy months. The fresh air wore them out and gave her thirty precious minutes of peace. Here the two girls entertained themselves with adventures on the playground and rarely found a moment to fight. She was amazed that Dr. Clark was the one who had suggested the place.

She had promised Billy to stay away from the park across town where the little girl was taken. Still, she remained alert as the girls chased one another. The playground was a multi-platformed structure with an upper level of monkey bars and walkways. Small landings offered three slides that spilled over the sides. One slide was an enclosed tube, and the other two were side by side and perfect for racing. Built off the side of the structure, a large beam held three swings. Three boys were in the grassy space to the left tossing a football. Laughter echoed all around, and Beth took a moment to size up the adults in the vicinity. There were several moms today, and two men with kids in tow. No single men wandering suspiciously.

Her attention was drawn back to her daughters. Maggie had climbed to the top of the structure, a princess trapped in a castle, while Esther was pretending to be a dragon, stomping and snorting around on the ground. They were telling each other what to say and mapping out the scene as they went along. These were moments Beth held in her heart. She smiled when she looked at them and pulled out her phone when a text alert sounded. It was only a moment.

A third voice joined in the make-believe play, and it drew Beth from the message that had come through. Just a reminder for an upcoming doctor's appointment. A young girl, maybe thirteen, Beth surmised, had joined the girls. Her dark hair was pulled up into two puffs. Her jeans had fashionable rips in them. Beth watched, closely assessing the situation. Alarms rang as she recounted the story Billy had shared about the kids leading other kids away. *That park was on the other side of town, though…* After a few minutes, she decided the girl seemed harmless enough, sweet even, yet she continued to watch the girls play.

After a few minutes, Maggie ran to Beth, telling her all about their new friend.

"Her name is Missy," Maggie said breathlessly. The cold was evident from Maggie's pink cheeks and watery eyes. Her jacket was unzipped and her hat askew. Beth adjusted both jacket and hat as Maggie filled her in. One pantleg was pulled out from her new yellow rubber rain boots. Beth had just found matching jackets and rain boots today. The girls were excited, and Beth was grateful for the sale price.

"She said she lives around the corner. She likes to play pretend, like me and Esther. She's really nice, Mama. She said she could be our new friend."

Beth finished by tucking Maggie's hair behind her ears under the hat, then fixing the wayward pant leg. "There, now you're all ready to go back to play. I'm so glad your friend is nice. You must stay where I can see you."

Beth glanced away from Maggie to take note of Esther. Her heart leaped to her throat. Instantly she was half-standing. She grabbed Maggie by the hand. The playground was busy, but she did not see Esther. Or their new friend.

"I don't see your sister." She hurried onto the mulch floor in search of her girl, Maggie in tow.

"Mama, where is Esther?" Maggie asked, her voice shaky.

Fields of Gomorrah

"I'm sure she's on the slide or something. Come on, let's go see ..." Beth frantically scanned the park. She heard a muffled cry from somewhere ... or was that her imagination?

She caught a glimpse of Esther's white jacket on the other side of the playground and breathed a sigh of relief. She hadn't even realized she had been holding her breath in. Still unsettled, she raced to the tubular slide so she could caution Esther not to stray out of her sight.

However, by the time Beth arrived at the slide, there was again no sign of her little one. She began to panic and beat back the fear. She was instantly in prayer and drew out her cell phone to call Billy.

"Billy, I can't find Esther. We are at the park—No. You told me to stay away from that one. I'm not far from the house. Billy, listen—a girl came, Maggie was telling me, and now I can't find Esther." Her words were as jumbled as her thoughts. It would have helped if Billy hadn't interrupted her. The world was spinning around her. She was rushing from slides to swings, trying to catch even a glimpse of her child.

Drawing the attention and help of the other parents, Beth's voice was high and trembled as she called out Esther's name.

Billy shouted from the phone, "Beth! Please! Calm down, and tell me what is going on. What do you mean you can't find Esther?"

Looking down at her oldest, Beth's heart broke when she saw the fear in her child's eyes. Fear that reflected her own. She did her best to focus on relaying the facts to her husband. "Billy. We came to the park. A young girl, maybe thirteen, started playing with the girls." Tears began streaming down Beth's face as she wrestled with the looming possibility even as she was describing it. Dread filled her with its heavy weight as she realized this was the same pattern Billy had described. *But that park was on the other side of town.* "She came and started playing with the girls. Maggie must have seen me watching, and she came over to tell me about her—"

"No, Mama. She sent me over."

Beth slowly turned her entire body to face her child. "What, honey?" Her voice barely a whisper, she was unable to maintain a calm, even tone.

175

"Renata sent me over. She said to go tell you how nice she was and to tell you that she was my new friend." Maggie's bottom lip began to tremble. Beth took her hand.

"Did you hear that, Billy?" Beth's hand was shaking as she held the phone. She turned away from Maggie, hoping to shield her daughter from her expression. She felt all but certain now that Esther had been taken.

"Yes, I heard. Beth. Tell me every detail you can remember about this girl."

Once he went into detective mode, any reserve Beth had was gone. She knelt and drew a weeping Maggie toward her chest and allowed the sobs to roll over her.

Thirty-Six

A cool breeze swept into the room as the door opened and several new arrivals were ushered in. Observing what she could about each child, Cassie made mental notes that she would later jot down in her Bible.

There were only four of them today.

Since the day Draven had come and selected Missy, she had changed. Very rarely was she the girl Cassie had first met. There were moments she seemed to be having conversations with invisible people. Her mood was erratic at best, and she had vile reactions whenever she saw Cassie praying. It was as though she had become … *possessed*. Cassie shuddered at the thought, wondering more about her story of Renata.

Returning her attention back to the arrivals, Cassie refused to dwell on the thoughts forming in her mind. The first child, a boy about nine years old, came through sullen yet defiant. A black eye and swollen lip were evidence of the fight he had put up—and lost. His dark hair was a tousled mess hanging over his face. He wore jeans that were too big and a ripped T-shirt. It appeared to Cassie that he had rummaged through some donations before he was captured. *He should have stayed at whatever shelter he had found.* The next two girls were older than Cassie. She was surprised. Having been the oldest for so long, she was shocked to realize she felt threatened by them. What if one of them tried to take over guarding the children?

When her eyes landed on the little girl with Missy, she stopped. There was something about this frightened little girl that Cassie felt compelled to protect. Missy had her arm around the child's shoulder, not in a protective way but more … territorial. Cassie knew she would have to fight to protect this little one.

The guards went through the normal routine. All too familiar with it now, Cassie kept a close eye on the older girls. They stuck together, huddled in the corner, crying on one another's shoulders. It dawned on Cassie that they might be sisters. She turned her attention to the little girl and watched as Missy roughly shoved the child as they walked to the corner. Crying out in pain, she fell to her knees after one of Missy's more aggressive prods.

"I want my mama," she wailed, stomping in her yellow boots and drawing her jacket close.

"She's gone," Missy snarled. "I'm your mama now. Take off that jacket." The little one shrank back against the wall and whimpered.

Cassie was impressed with the courage of the little one as she put up a fight and refused to remove the coat. "No! I won't take it off. My mama gave it to me. I'll never take it off!"

Cassie got up and walked over to Missy and her new charge.

Missy saw her coming and stepped in front of the child. "She's mine. Go back to yours." Her chin jutted forward, and she planted her hands on her hips in defiance. The little girl slid down the wall to land softly on her bottom, tears streaming down her face.

"None of them belong to us," Cassie said firmly. "We just need to do our best to care for one another." She looked down and smiled at the little girl. "What's your name, honey?"

The little girl stared at Cassie, looked up tentatively at Missy, then spoke softly. "Esther."

"Hello, Esther. I'm sure you're scared."

Her little face bunched up, as tears continued to roll down her ruddy cheeks. "I want my mommy." Her voice broke. She pulled her knees close to her chest, wrapped little hands around her yellow boots, and bowed her head.

Cassie stood up and stared Missy in the eyes. "Why did she come in with you?"

"Because she's mine. I told you that."

"We don't own each other, Missy. I told you that."

"Missy's gone. It's only Renata," she declared.

"No, that's not true. Missy is still with us. You have to let her speak." Cassie found courage she didn't know she had as she faced this demon head on.

"She won't come." The creature taunted. "I found the girl. I took the girl. The girl is mine now."

Esther began to cry louder. She was terrified. "Oh please, Jesus, help me!" She sobbed.

An odd sort of hissing came from Missy as she recoiled at the name of Jesus. Cassie knelt again to speak with Esther.

"You know Jesus?" she asked tenderly.

"He loves me. Mama talks to Him every day," Esther told her.

Cassie smiled. "He does. I'm sure your mom is talking to Him right now. Would you like to talk to Him, too?"

"I just did," she said, matter of fact. "You can if you want."

"I talk to Him all the time too."

"Knock it off." Missy interrupted, pushing Cassie off balance, forcing her back from Esther.

From where she fell on the floor, Cassie eyed her opponent. She knew Missy was still there. She didn't know how Missy had "found" this little girl, but Cassie was determined to protect her.

"Okay, so what if she wants to come with me?" Cassie challenged the spirit.

"She can't," Missy spat. "She's mine."

"Actually, she belongs to Jesus. You heard her." Cassie crossed her legs and motioned for the child to come to her, calling out the bluff of the enemy. Esther quickly scurried around Missy with a wary eye and hurried to Cassie.

Eyes wild and teeth bared, Missy could only snarl. She appeared incapable of even touching the child. Slowly, Cassie stood and walked with Esther back to her side of the rectangle room.

Cassie settled Esther among the little ones and asked her to share her story. She wrote down her name and age and the details the child could remember. Eventually, Cassie rocked her to sleep, and the girl slept fitfully for a few hours. Cassie knew she had to be exhausted after such an ordeal.

Father God, how am I going to keep this little one safe? I can't do it. You have to. You have to place a shield of protection over her. Do not let her be used by this evil world. Send our rescuer, Lord. Soon.

Thirty-Seven

Shaking her by the shoulders, Billy shouted her name. "Beth! Beth! Wake up! It's a nightmare. Please wake up." Beth opened her eyes, and tears filled them immediately.

Billy pulled her into his arms and held her tightly. "I will find her, Beth. I will find her if it's the last thing I do. We will not lose another child." Tears clouded his vision as he held his sobbing wife.

Billy struggled under the weight he had been avoiding since the loss of their son. He knew he had pushed Beth away. Her battle with depression was all the worse because he wasn't there to help her through it. He had failed in so many ways. He didn't want to see her fall again.

"I know. Oh Billy. I can't. God knows that I can't survive another …" Beth stopped talking abruptly, and Billy followed her eyes to see Maggie peeking from the door.

"Darling, you can come in." Beth gestured to her daughter and patted the bed. "Come here, honey."

Maggie raced across the carpeted floor and climbed up onto the king-size bed. She nestled against her mother. Beth cupped her chin and guided her face and looked her in the eye.

"It's okay, my love," she whispered and wiped away Maggie's tears.

Maggie nodded and silently wiped away Beth's with a tender touch.

Billy was touched by this moment between his wife and child yet filled with deep concern, as Maggie had not spoken since that awful day.

As Maggie nestled in next to her mother, she was soon asleep. Beth moved her to the middle of the bed.

Beth whispered fiercely, "I am so angry, Billy. How a child could take another. How she manipulated one sister against the other. And how I was tricked. I should know better. You warned me!" Her voice broke. "Now, I just want Maggie to know it wasn't her fault. It was mine."

With Maggie sleeping between them, Billy had to slip from the bed and walk around to sit behind Beth. She leaned into him, and he wrapped his arms around her.

"Beth, it was not your fault. And you have every right to be angry. I am too. I'm right here with you. We are in this together. I know when we lost William, I disappeared on you. I chose to lose myself in my work so I wouldn't have to face the grief. I haven't been there for you. I've been distant and removed. I'm so sorry." Billy's tears fell into her hair, and she wrapped her arms around his. "But you won't have to walk this alone, and I *will* find her. I will bring Esther home."

"I love you, Billy." she whispered.

"I love you too."

A few moments passed as they held each other. Billy looked down at his sleeping daughter. "I think it may be good to take Maggie to see Dr. Morrison. Let's see what he suggests."

"Yes." Beth ran a finger down Maggie's soft cheek. "I agree."

After parking the van, Beth climbed out and opened the door for Maggie. She offered her hand to help her out of the van. Then they walked toward the office together. Once inside, Beth guided Maggie to a chair in the waiting room that gave her a clear view of the TV. Beth went to speak with the receptionist.

Bridget greeted her with a sympathetic smile. "Hello, Mrs. Everett."

Beth knew she was a mess. She hadn't showered in days. There was no rest for her thoughts; always thinking of Esther. How scared was she? Was she safe? Was there someone to take care of her? She was tormented both night and day.

She nervously pulled at her hair, trying to set it to rights.

Bridget took her hand. "I am so sorry, Mrs. Everett. We are praying for Esther. Dr. Morrison will be ready for you in just a moment. Is there anything we can do for you?"

Beth was moved by the young woman's kindness. Tears welled in her eyes, and her throat burned. Surprised that she had any tears left to cry, she just shook her head softly and returned to Maggie.

She let Maggie crawl into her lap. She promised herself for the millionth time since she was born that her baby would never be too big to sit in her lap. She breathed in the scent of Maggie's hair and ran her fingers tenderly across her back. Her daughter relaxed and leaned against Beth as they waited.

The nurse called them and led them back to the room. Beth sat in the guest chair and motioned for Maggie to climb onto the exam table. Instead, Maggie moved into her mother's lap, refusing to sit by herself. "I know you miss Esther, baby. Of course you can sit in my lap."

Beth was taken aback when the brief knock on the door was followed by the arrival of Dr. Clark. She wore a brightly colored tunic dress under her stark white lab coat. The space was tight in the exam room. She pulled out the wheeled chair from behind the computer stand and sat knee to knee with Beth.

"Oh! Hello, ladies. I'm so sorry. I thought this was my room." Dr. Clark settled across from Beth and Maggie disregarding the fact that this was not her room. Softly, she spoke directly to Maggie. "How are you, Maggie? You must be so sad. Even though your sister is missing, I'm sure you'll be ready to play at the park again in no time."

Maggie buried her face in her mother's shoulder. Bristling, Beth sat up a little straighter and pulled her arms more tightly around her daughter.

"Really, Dr. Clark. We are here to see Dr. Morrison. I hardly understand why you are here." Beth's tone was sharp. She simply did not have the emotional space to deal with this woman. Though their last meeting had been civil, she had no desire to continue with her.

"Take it easy, Mrs. Everett." The smile she offered didn't touch her eyes. Her brows furrowed and her mouth fell into a thin line. "I just wanted to check in, to see how Maggie is doing."

"That is actually why we are here to see *Dr. Morrison*." Beth stressed in frustration that this woman continued to intrude upon her family.

"Yes, well, I understand you are going through a devastating event. Esther is a sweet girl; it must be tearing you apart."

Her false compassion stirred fire in Beth's heart. Her face flushed, and her eyes grew bright. Before she could say anything, the woman was standing and moving the chair back into place, turning her back on Beth.

"Of course, I don't mean to intrude. I'm sure she will be found soon. Certainly, those yellow boots and coat stand out."

There was a quick knock on the door, and Dr. Morrison entered. Frowning when he saw Dr. Clark, he crossed his arms.

"Oh! Dr. Morrison! I'm so sorry," she stammered. "The nurse must've put the wrong flag out. I thought this was my patient. So sorry! Excuse me, please." She quickly exited, her broad figure pushing against Dr. Morrison in her haste.

"My apologies, Mrs. Everett," Dr. Morrison said, once Dr. Clark had exited.

Beth's mouth was still open from the shock of the woman's lies. Beth was certain she knew exactly what she was doing. She shook her head and took the doctor's extended hand.

"Quite all right, Doctor. I'm just offended by her. Why does it seem as though she seeks us out every time we come here?" Beth asked, her voice strained.

"Well, I know our profession is not one-size-fits-all. Dr. Clark connects well with many of her patients. She tells me it grieves her that she got off on the wrong foot with you, and in her admittedly awkward way, she is trying to make things right."

"I understand, and I appreciate that. But I really must ask that she stay away from us. Our concerns need to be taken into consideration, or I will have to leave this office. And my girls are just so ..." Beth faltered as she spoke. *My girls. But Esther isn't here.* Throat constricting, Beth felt the familiar burn. "They are both so comfortable with you, Dr. Morrison."

He nodded. "Again, I'm so sorry. I can't imagine all that you are dealing with right now. How can I help Maggie today?

Beth swiped at the tears as they began to fall and took a few deep breaths. "It's that, well, Maggie hasn't felt like talking since ..."

Turning to Maggie, Dr. Morrison offered a bright smile. "Maggie, tell me how you are doing?"

Maggie just stared at him. He altered his words. "Maggie, are you doing okay?"

She started with a nod but turned it into a shake.

"Is there anything you would like to talk about?"

She shook her head more solidly. Turning around, she buried her face in Beth's shoulder.

"I think you can give her some time," Dr. Morrison advised. "I'm sure you are both in need of processing everything. So long as Maggie understands that this is not her fault."

Maggie turned her face ever so slightly toward the doctor.

He added, "And that she is safe."

Beth realized he had addressed the two main burdens that Maggie was likely carrying. She felt her daughter relax in her arms.

"Thank you, Doctor," Beth said with a sigh.

Maggie offered a thumbs-up.

Beth smiled. At least it was interaction. Dr. Morrison clapped his hands, as a smile splashed across his face.

"That's a girl, Maggie." He turned to Beth. "Let's check back in a couple of weeks, to see how things are going. If she is talking and able to share some of her fears, then we are on the right road."

"Okay, that sounds good." Beth's tone was a little lighter; hope had broken in.

Stacey Herring

As they walked back to the car, Maggie was still silent, but Beth was encouraged. Soon lost in thought as she ruminated over their encounter with Dr. Clark, Beth's heart was stabbed by fear. *Why did she say something to Maggie about the park?* Beth reasoned within herself. *That is just so callous.*

She loaded Maggie into her seat in the van and helped her buckle in. Climbing in behind the steering wheel, she set her purse in the passenger seat. A distant thought nagged at her, but she couldn't quite place it. It was a disconcerted feeling, a slight anxiety. Then, like lightning it struck her heart. Beth knew Billy had released the yellow jacket as a detail in the missing child case, but *how did she know Esther was wearing yellow boots?*

Thirty-Eight

Later that day Beth had pushed herself to go to the Bible study with Melody and Mae. Although she went to the park every day in search of her child, today's visits were the first Beth had had since Esther's kidnapping.

Tomorrow it would be a week since her daughter was taken. Each day brought a struggle to function. Maggie had become her focus. Melody had set her up in the living room with a peanut butter and jelly sandwich and cartoons. Still, the darkness of depression threatened to take Beth again. The man hunt had turned up no evidence. She was terrified for her child.

The three ladies sat at Melody's kitchen table. Fading bruises still showed signs of Melody's attack, and Beth was broken, staring into space. She realized she was becoming numb to the emotions that had plagued her for days.

Beth caught the glance that Melody and Mae exchanged. She shifted in her chair and tried to engage.

"What delicious treat did you bring this time, Mae?" Beth asked.

Mae got up from the table, moved to the counter, and began to prepare the cake she had brought with her. "Pineapple upside-down cake—my husband's favorite. He was not so happy to see it leave the house! This will help you build some energy. Melody, will you pour the coffee?" Mae balanced a large piece of the cake on the knife before it fell topside down on the plate. She flipped it over with two fingers and moved onto the next slice.

She sat the decadent dessert in front of Beth and Melody as the women sat in silence.

"I can't believe you were attacked," Beth offered, coming back to the present moment. "I'm so sorry."

"It was terrifying." Melody's hand trembled as she set a cup of coffee in front of Beth. "My bruises are healing, but I am struggling with such fear. We went out the next day and bought a new washing machine."

Beth wrestled with compassion for her friend who had survived her ordeal, while she was forced to wonder and worry over her missing child.

"I haven't stopped praying for Esther." She placed a hand on Beth's shoulder. Beth bit her lip as tears raced down her face, and she held back a sob.

"I just am trying to work through this." Beth shook her head as despair filled her again. "I am fighting a loss of faith. I am angry at God for allowing this. I'm angry at myself for being tricked. The wounds were just healing from baby Will and now this …" Her voice broke. "I don't know how I will survive. I keep dreaming of the field, the girl, the baby … Now Esther has joined them." Her shoulders shook as sobs overtook her.

Melody grabbed a box of tissues and placed it in front of her friend. Then she took one for herself. Mae pulled out three and blew her nose.

"Then," Beth started as she pulled a tissue from the box, "the strangest thing happened at the doctor's office this morning." She took a deep ragged breath and shared the story of Dr. Clark's interruption. "But she commented on Esther's yellow boots. I had just bought those the day she went missing. How would the doctor know what Esther was wearing? It was a detail that Billy hadn't released."

"You need to tell him that," Melody stated. "She gives me the creeps. From what you've shared about her, I would definitely say she's a suspect."

"You're right. I guess Billy and I have been processing so much on our own … he and I haven't really spoken."

"Well, I'll read between those lines and ask the hard questions," Mae declared, tapping her manicured nails against the table as she leaned toward Beth. "Why aren't you speaking?"

"It's just opened so much of our past. Baby Will mostly. But then, this morning—he shared some of what he has been struggling with. I can tell he's afraid I'm going to slip away again." Beth allowed her tears now. "But I can't do that. I won't do that. Esther needs me. Maggie needs me."

"Billy needs you," Melody said softly. "It's at times like these that the enemy would love nothing more than to destroy you both. To pit you against each other. Be careful not to blame one another, or yourselves. This tragedy is not your fault, and it's not his. Your strength to withstand will come when you both lean on each other and stay focused on God."

Thirty-Nine

Things were changing. The guards were more tense, the visitors less frequent. No one had been sent on a job for weeks. Cassie felt the winds of change, and hope began to blossom. She calmed herself with the reality that she was still captive, she had no contacts, and all she could do was write down as many details as possible in the Bible—and comfort the brokenhearted children.

And she was showing.

The changes in her body were evident. She was surprised by the tenacity she felt to protect the child. Although the innocent child in her womb had been forced upon her, she was unable to blame the actions of the father on him or her. She was terrified. She knew what happened when girls got pregnant here. They were forcibly removed and returned, without the child, in just a few hours. The pain they endured was ghastly. Sometimes they bled for days and were drugged even longer.

She prayed with fervor. "Dear Jesus, please protect this baby. Protect me."

James burst through the door, tears streaming down his face. He stumbled to Cassie and knelt to pull her into his arms. She stood, confused and scared at the commotion.

"Please, Ethan!" He wept bitterly as Ethan strode in after him. "This is different. This is my child. Don't take it away."

He spoke as if it was a puppy he was asking for. His child-mind could not contemplate all that he had done.

"Do you even realize the position you've put me in, James" Ethan's tone was bitter. "The money I will lose, what I have to tell Draven?" He was clearly furious with his brother.

Ethan motioned to the guards, who came and pulled Cassie away from James. As they dragged her from the rectangle room, her fears toppled over in her mind. Her body went limp. Her panic was palpable, but even in the slow-motion, surreal moment, she knew any attempt at escape would be futile. Her throat burning with tears and tight against emotion, she labored to move with the guards, hoping against hope that the process would take her life along with her child.

Cassie was bewildered as she was led through a parking garage and up a service elevator. Confusion was her guide as they freely walked through the open office space, then down rows of cubicles with uniform desks and computers. Filled with men and women punching away at the keys. Did no one think it suspicious that a pregnant teen was walking through the room by armed men?

But few even looked up from their computers.

One woman, large and boisterous, was at the water cooler. Cassie's heart leapt ... *She saw me. I know she saw me. She looked right at me.*

Although she watched Cassie being escorted along the aisle between desks, she didn't move from her place. She seemed almost frozen, in fact.

The men walked her into Ethan's office. She knew it was his office as he was just rounding the corner of his desk, pushing the intercom.

"Mrs. Murphy." He paused, waiting for a response. "Mrs. Murphy, are you there?" More impatiently.

"Uh. Yes, yes sir. I'm here. Was that your, um, your niece?" she asked breathlessly.

Cassie wondered if it was the same woman, she had seen at the water cooler.

"Actually, she is one of our success stories with Homeless Humanity. And I will not be interrupted for the next hour. Please see to it that any calls and visitors are held."

"Yes, sir. Of course."

"Have a seat." Turning his attention back to Cassie, Ethan directed her to have a seat.

She looked at the men still holding her arms. "Would you let me go then?" She addressed them sharply.

They obliged, and she slid down into the black leather chair opposite Ethan's massive desk.

The office reflected his personality. Cold, hard lines of contemporary furniture. No pictures: nothing that would reveal any personal detail or preference.

"Are you curious as to what Homeless Humanity is?" he asked her. She did not respond yet held his gaze. *What is his game? Why take me from the room?*

He continued. "It's my program to assist the homeless. Provide them housing, give them life skills, job training, and restore them into society." His smile was broad. Cassie felt a shiver creep down her spine. She was to be paraded in plain sight of his company. Rooms full of people that couldn't see her for what she truly was—a victim walking in the open.

"Do you know who loves the idea? The pretentious rich." A derisive laugh punctuated the statement. "Those fools with so much surplus they choose to invest in unproven programs that make them feel righteous. Little do they know the program feeds the supply chain for the dark and depraved. Don't get me wrong; some of my highest donors are my best customers, but most have no idea what their tax write-off truly funds." He stood and looked out the large glass window behind his desk. "It never was what I wanted to do. But with Draven …

"James is like a child," he abruptly changed the subject, as he pulled his phone from his pocket. "He was thrown against the wall as a child and

192

suffered great damage to mind and body." He turned back to his desk but didn't look at her as he spoke, scrolling instead through his phone.

Cassie gasped at his bluntness.

"He has no idea what he has done, what it will cost me. And you. He has the misconception that you can live a happily-ever-after life." He looked at her directly. "We both know that's not possible." Ethan pulled a pen from the leather holder on his desk pad and jotted something down on a sticky note.

Still Cassie remained silent. She was evaluating the situation. The guards. The door. The space. Again, no hope of escape. But if that secretary saw her … Hope persisted.

"Our mother was kind but foolish." He pulled his chair out and sat down. "She brought men into the home who were vile and violent. She entertained them by making rent, to put food on the table. I carried on that role for a while in my youth."

He rolled up his sleeve and referenced the brand. Cassie looked from the brand and then held his eyes. He broke their gaze and pulled his sleeve back down. "I vowed never to be taken advantage of again. I worked hard, made the right connections, and built this business from the ground up. What the world sees is but the tip of the iceberg. What happens underground is hidden from the population at large. All they need is a few success stories. A happy, well-adjusted teen, a homeless man's makeover and reunification to society, a business that provides both work and success to the 'least of these.'" He sketched air quotes with a snide look of contempt. "And under it all, that frail fabric of our society, my real business grows."

She shivered in her chair, just beginning to piece together why he would risk bringing her to the office. Because he could.

"But you. You are different. James, in his innocence, sees something good in you. Connects with you somehow. You remind him of our mother, perhaps. You're strong. The guards tell me you don't complain, though they have provoked you. You shelter the children. I want to ask you—to what avail? What purpose does it fulfill? They will all end up like you, like so many before you. Lost children that disappear into darkness." He stood and walked to the front of his desk. With him so close, she instinctively shrank back into her chair.

He leaned against the hard dark glass and evaluated her. "You're not much to look at, really. Young and pretty, sure. But ... not memorable. Your first job you almost screwed up. I almost had you killed that night. I should have."

Cassie watched him, never lowering her eyes off his. She held his gaze in a challenge she had no idea she was capable of. She knew her life was in God's hands, not his. If he didn't kill her that night, it wasn't because of him. Then a smile, soft and slow, tugged and teased the corners of her mouth, and it provoked Ethan.

"I don't understand you. So many have come through my business. Some of them now work for me. You met Amber. And Melvin. This business makes you strong. You learn to take life instead of giving it. You turn on your hunters, and like primitive man, you kill without remorse."

Her smile faded. He was either psychotic or delusional. "That's not how it works." She spoke barely above a whisper. "That's not how it has to be."

"Oh?" he asked, amusement lilting his voice. "Really, so you think you can have happily ever after?"

"Not like this. Not with James. Not in this ... business." She didn't even try to hide the disgust she felt.

James came into the room unannounced, and Ethan just watched as he ambled in. "My patience grows thin, brother." He sighed, standing straight and tall.

"I just want her," James said. "She told me about J-Jesus—"

"I made a promise to our mother, James." Ethan talked over his brother. Cassie couldn't tell if he didn't hear his brother or just ignored him. "She died in a pool of her own blood, brutally beaten by the same man who destroyed you. I held her in my arms as she died, and I promised her I would care for you. And I have."

He walked over to his brother as he spoke. His voice was strained, his eyes narrow.

"But now, you bring me this. You interfered. You made things ... complicated. And it's time for you to clean up the mess. You know the process. You know what we do in these situations. The doctor's number is on my desk. James, you need to call. You need to make the arrangements. You need to fix this." He ended with a finger pointing at Cassie.

"B-but you said I could have her," James stammered, wiping the snot from his nose with the back of his dirty sleeve. "I could have her, and she would be mine. So this baby is mine."

"No. James." The tension in his tone could slice through stone.

Yet it seemed to fall on deaf ears. Cassie flinched as he slapped his brother across the face.

Ethan stormed back to his desk and picked up the phone. He punched in the numbers. "This is protocol, James. It is what we do here. She will see the doctor, and when she returns, you will not touch her again until I say so. Understood?"

"Please, Ethan—"

James's plea was cut short when the door swung open, and Draven stepped into the office. He adjusted his tie and stood in the center of the room.

Mae arrived behind him, hands on her hips, "My apologies, Ethan. Mr. Wolfe refused to—"

"It's fine, Mrs. Murphy. Please return to your desk." Ethan waved her off. She slowly retreated. *I know she saw me this time. She is paying attention.* Cassie dared to hope.

James immediately retreated to the corner, cowering in fear. Ethan looked up from his desk with a dour expression on his face, obviously annoyed by the intrusion. Cassie tried to disappear into the chair, slinking down and trying to remain small.

"Ethan," Draven said curtly, "I have heard there is a development with one of the girls." He saw Cassie in the chair and gestured rudely in her direction. "Is it this one?"

"Yes, Draven." Ethan had turned back to the task at hand and didn't bother to look up from his computer. However, he ended the call in mid-ring. He spoke as if it were yet another mundane, annoying task he had to attend to in the multitude of mundane things he managed on a daily basis. "The girl is pregnant." He waved a hand toward Cassie. "I will have it fixed by the end of the day. This isn't anything new—"

"No, you won't. She will come to term, and we will have the baby." Draven spoke with pompous authority as he moved to the seat beside Cassie. Her heart raced both from his proximity and his words. *I'll be able to have this baby!*

Ethan and James simultaneously raised their heads to look at Draven.

"What?" exclaimed Ethan. "What do you mean, 'we'? This is my business, Draven. I decide what happens. And we do not deal in babies." Ethan's eyes narrowed.

Cassie's hope plummeted at Ethan's words. *Deal in babies ... what did he mean?*

Draven only smiled. He crossed his lanky legs and leaned back in the chair looking at Cassie. Her spirit wilted. Dark evil emanated from this man. She was frozen with fear as he reached over and stroked her arm. Inwardly, she cringed at his touch, eager to wash her arm.

"Draven, this is my business, and we always abort the fetus," Ethan stated. "Why would this be different? Please explain to me why I should take on this burden and lose one of my girls for months?"

Draven cocked his head to one side, seemingly about to share some details with Ethan, but in the end all he offered was "She appears close to term, so it won't be for long. I have a plan, and that is all you need to know." He uncrossed his legs and stood to his full height, dismissing Ethan's objections and instantly stripping away any authority he thought he had over the situation.

"Return her to the group, and place Missy to oversee her. Harriet is firm on this."

"Harriet is—" Ethan shook his head.

Cassie couldn't read if it was frustration or disbelief, but she was busy processing the instructions and what it would mean for her. Missy in charge of her. Cassie felt her body begin to tremble.

"I don't place girls in charge. It's not a hierarchy. That just creates chaos." Ethan was firm. "No. The guards will be in charge."

Cassie released her breath slowly. Having Missy in charge of her with any amount of authority would be terrifying. She was thankful for Ethan's wounded ego.

Draven shrugged his shoulders. "Well, you will need someone to be with her when she goes into labor. We will need to be notified immediately. We will need to manage that carefully. I would think the guards have better things to do." With that he left the office.

Ethan sat staring out the window in silence for some time. Cassie didn't dare make a move and hardly let herself breathe. Unsure what Ethan would decide, once again she realized her fate clearly seemed to be in his hands.

He turned in his chair and looked at Cassie for a moment. Then he picked up the phone. He punched in some numbers as he said, "A chain is only as strong as its weakest link."

Forty

Cassie dutifully obeyed when Ethan motioned for her to remain silent. He placed the phone on the speaker. "James, I need you to go home." James nodded and scuffled obediently out the door.

"Ethan." Harriet sounded almost pleased to hear him. Cassie recognized her gravelly tone immediately. "What has you calling me?" Cassie could hear her fingers tapping against a keyboard.

"I understand I am to place Missy in charge of the pregnant girl."

Her smug tone was clear. "Who told you that?" She chuckled.

Ethan was silent for a moment. He stood and began to pace. "Draven. He met the girl today and said you were adamant that Missy oversees her. I don't place girls in charge. What's your reason?"

Cassie flinched at the reference to herself. How callously he spoke of her.

"Yes," Harriet confirmed. "It just makes sense, doesn't it? Missy has proven to be loyal. And she came to us willingly. You can't say that about all the girls. Especially the pregnant one. I can see a lot of promise in Missy and feel we can mold her in ways that will meet our needs."

"James is the father. Draven said he didn't want any loose ends with a father around."

"How did you let that happen?" Harriet exclaimed.

Ethan walked to the fish tank, talking over her. "How do you know Missy will actually help the situation?"

Harriet paused. "I don't think I have to explain myself to you. But we do need someone who will be attentive to her to fulfill the plan effectively."

Ethan tapped softly on the glass. "Right, it would make sense. Because we need the baby to be free of any legal ties. So there would be no hospital …"

"Legal ties? Is that what he told you? That is something Draven would say." She sounded irritated. "Legal ties don't matter when you have a child whose existence is never reported. And it's not going to live long enough to matter to the law anyway. The baby just needs to arrive on the twentieth by midnight."

Cassie covered her mouth as a soft gasp escaped, and an ominous foreboding encircled her heart.

The tapping of keys on her keyboard resumed with ferocity. "But yes, a hospital is out of the question. I will be the one delivering the child. You'll need to make arrangements for her to be there on time."

"Of course," Ethan continued. Cassie prayed he was just stringing her along to garner the details, but with her child's life the subject of discussion, she struggled to maintain any sense of calm. Her hands began to flex as the familiar panic set in.

"At the Wisdom Foundation? And the girl would be back to work when, exactly?"

He seemed to understand where the plan was going, but Cassie wasn't following along.

"Never." Harriet scoffed. "Didn't Draven share this with you? She will be a bonus part of the sacrifice, though it's the baby that will be the greatest gift to the master." She let out a gleeful laugh.

Ethan recoiled, dropping the phone onto the tiled floor and covering Cassie's raw objection as she covered her womb. She tried to choke back the sound. She was starting to feel faint as the information registered.

He quickly retrieved the phone and discovered the screen was shattered. "I'm sorry, Harriet, that was my secretary. She tends to interrupt—" He walked back to his desk and slid into his chair, jotted some notes down in his planner.

"Tell her to leave! I swear there is nothing more frustrating than a nosy secretary." Harriet huffed.

"Yes, that is what I did. Harriet, I have to go. I just wanted you to give me the clarification on Missy." Ethan spoke quickly as he ended the call.

He sat frozen at his desk, while Cassie, no longer able to hold back the floodgate of emotions, wept uncontrollably. His face paled.

Slowly, he turned to face the massive window and the city that lay before him, muttering to himself. Cassie restrained her emotions to hear him. Her sobbing dwindled to soft hiccups, and her breathing remained ragged. "I thought I was in charge. This was my city. I know everything about this town. I ran the dark streets myself, finding food, stealing, selling drugs, selling myself. I survived. I took care of my brother. And now what am I doing?"

He turned from the window and looked at Cassie. She wiped her eyes. "Please do not let them do this, Ethan. This child is your blood." She realized the one connection that might matter to him was the child she now carried.

He seemed to be wrestling within himself. "I knew this would not end well. James." He ground out the name through clenched teeth. "If I send you to the doctor, or I let them take the child, either way my issues are solved. But—"

Cassie prayed with fervency. *Please, Lord. Please reach through this darkness and rescue me.*

"I'll send you back for now. I'll keep Amber in charge of you. Harriet won't make one decision over my business." He paused again. "Sacrifice? What have I gotten involved in? Draven told me he would invest in my business. Instead, I am building one for him, one I swore I would never be a part of. What can I do now? My hands have bloodstains. His are clean."

Forty-One

Billy sat in the small office with the chief and Detectives Malik and Wright, as well as his partner, Dixon. Malik and Wright, as usual, were seated in the two chairs facing the desk. Billy and Dixon stood leaning against filing cabinets.

Billy knew he looked ragged and slightly disheveled and that the pressure of the last few weeks was apparent in his face. He knew he shouldn't even be on this case, as it was his daughter who was missing, and there had been enough connections to consider her case linked to his own.

Once again, he ran through the information he had received from Cassie on that dark night. Amir Malik and Paul Wright were there to share what they had learned from speaking with Ethan a few days ago.

"Yes," Billy repeated, "she described Lily: blond hair, blue eyes, age seven. Even confirmed the name. She said there were nearly thirty more in what she called 'the rectangle room.' The informant—who we presume is Ethan's brother, James—told us to look for shipping containers. That matches up with her description. This girl … she was terrified and yet, so brave. She could have run in the chaos we created, but she chose to stay and protect the children. She's a fighter.

"She mentioned several other details. She said Draven has been to the location." Billy noticed Dixon shifting uncomfortably. "And a 'fat woman.' Not much of a description.

"Do we have any gang symbols for Ouroboros? I keep seeing that symbol pop up—a snake in a circle eating its own tail. Cassie said there was a symbol like that on the container, and several of the clients had similar tattoos."

"No." Amir spoke up. "Not a gang symbol. But it could be something more sinister." He paused long enough to warrant Billy pushing him to continue.

"What do you mean, Amir? More sinister. We are obviously dealing with evil here." Billy was tired, his daughter was missing, likely caught up in this human trafficking case, and these men were holding back information. The minutes ticked by, and he could feel the burden to find and free them. He could feel his fury building and did his best to restrain himself.

"We've been watching some members of the community." Amir paused again. "Some in trusted professions—teachers, doctors ..."

Chief Stone nodded, instructing him to continue.

"Even some cops. There are satanic groups meeting—"

Billy watched as Dixon shifted uncomfortably with a slight flush to his face. "I mean, it's a religion, right?" Dixon weakly objected. "I'm just saying, we need to be careful as we proceed here. They may be untraditional, but they have rights."

Pulling his eyes from Dixon, Amir resumed. "Anyway, yes, they have rights, I know. But what I was saying is that they meet regularly. At one location, there is a symbol similar to the Ouroboros. It's a small decal on the door of the Wisdom Foundation on Twenty-First and Elm. It's in the strip mall, next to Chandler's Fish Market and Benny's Pizzeria."

"Yeah, I found that early on in the investigation." Billy leafed through the papers in the file. "Here it is. Yeah, it's modernized, right? Couple of arrows instead of a snake."

Malik nodded. "Yes, that's right."

"Okay, that's a good lead. What do we know about the Wisdom Foundation?" He scanned his notes. "There is barely anything online about them, but what I do know is they are into New Age. And their CEO is—"

"Draven Wolfe," Amir and Billy said simultaneously.

Amir nodded in Billy's direction and continued, "Well, we know they meet in the evening. Seems that the folks all have daytime jobs, like I said, doctors, teachers ... you know, regular people. We know their clientele list includes a pediatrician, a chef, a former professor, and recently, we have seen Draven Wolfe in attendance."

Malik watched Dixon as he shared the last point.

Billy could barely stay in his seat. "What are we waiting for? We need to find this unit with the serpent. Maybe they marked more than just one."

Malik turned his attention to Billy. "This is the first we've learned of the connection, Billy. We need some time to find the containers."

"How hard could that be?" he retorted. It seemed Malik was pushing off the simplest solution.

"Billy, look, nearly twelve million containers arrive in the US every day. We have about fifteen million in our city alone. People are using them for housing, for storage—it's not just companies anymore. It's beyond construction site usage. We would have to look at each one individually. It's a good lead, but we need to make the connection to Wolfe. We still don't know the tie between Ethan and Wolfe."

Billy slumped at that, deflated. "We could have at least rescued the kids from the party. We could have followed their van."

Chief Stone spoke up. "Ethan split off from the kids. We want to find the connection so we can eliminate the entire operation. What we need is to find out how they are getting the units. Once we have the ties to the purchases, we can get the addresses."

"So, while these kids—possibly my own daughter—are subject to God knows what, we are supposed to be running through business receipts? You've got to be kidding me!"

Billy's outburst was met with complete silence. Chief Stone cleared his throat, "Billy, you need to rest. You've been living and breathing this case for weeks. You need some distance. Go home. Come back tomorrow."

Billy brushed off the offer, not about to slow down. "No, Chief. I'm fine. I've got this."

The chief held Billy's gaze. "I'm not suggesting it, Billy. It's an order. You need to keep a clear head on this. It's against my better judgment to keep you on this case. But I know how much you have invested. Go home. Come back tomorrow." His command left no room to argue.

Billy stood and crossed the room, fuming. He couldn't believe the chief would send him home when they were so close. He managed to grunt out an agreement in obedience to his supervisor but shut the door a bit too hard. He needed to get out and sift through the information he had. There had to be something he was missing.

Billy stormed into the house and threw his notebook across the office, making a crash that caused Beth to call out in surprise. "Is everything okay?" she asked.

"Yeah, yeah. The chief wanted me to come home and disconnect for a bit." He stepped into the living room and dropped the work file on the recliner. He yanked off his jacket and tossed it on the chair back and began to pace.

She smiled, wiping her hands on a towel. "Well, finally something the chief and I agree on."

He turned away.

"Why?" she asked.

"Said I need some distance from this case and to keep a clear head. I agree on the clear head. I know I'm missing something, Beth. I just don't know what. And every minute it takes me is a minute Esther stays out there!" He ran his hands through his hair in frustration.

He carried on a conversation with himself. "I can't find a fresh lead. I can't find my daughter. God, why did You allow this to happen? How can I fix it?"

"Billy, if you need to take a—"

"Don't say it, Beth. I can't take a break. I need to figure this out. I have to find them. I have to find Esther." He sat down and stared into space. He barely looked at Beth. Biting her lip, she remained silent as she picked up his file and sat down in her chair.

"What makes you think the cases are related?" She broke the silence.

"It's just a hunch right now, but there is something there. I just can't find it. The kids taking kids is a huge similarity, but I can't find the connection." He banged his fist against the coffee table.

"Billy, I wanted to tell you something about the pediatrician ..." She hesitated.

"Again with the doctor? I get it, babe. You don't like her." Billy retrieved the file from her and began pulling out items from the file and spreading them on the table, looking, searching for that missing detail. "Then don't take the girls to see her." He felt himself slip into old routines. Heard the way he spoke to his wife, looked up to see her wilt.

"I know you are upset, *William*. But you need to remember that I am too. I am struggling with this. It brings everything about baby William right back to the front. Only this time, I can't blame fate. I was the one with her at the park. I was the one who took my eyes off her. I was the one who lost her." She broke. Her eyes brimmed with tears, her shoulders shook, and she slumped back in the chair.

"Listen, Beth, I'm sorry. I don't blame you. No one blames you. It is not your fault that she's missing. What did you want to tell me about Dr. Clark?" He encouraged her yet remained distant. He wanted to go to her, but his old habits held him back. *Stay strong. Emotion equals weakness.* If he gave way to one, he was afraid the whole dam would burst.

"Well, does it stand to reason that I am questioning everything now?" She started looking at the images on the table. "What is that ring?" she asked. Her tone was odd, almost constricted.

He nodded. "Evidence from one of the missing girls. It does make sense for you to question everything. God knows I am. So what is it?" This time he was sincere. He retrieved his notebook from her and pulled out a pen.

Beth seemed to struggle to pull her eyes away from the image. She began to fidget again, but finally returned to her story. "She did impose herself again. It's not that I don't *like* her, Billy. It's that I don't *trust* her. This time she came in and started talking to Maggie. When Dr. Morrison came in, she bold-faced lied to him about why she was in the exam room." She was sitting up now, heat flushing her face as she rehashed the situation. Her eyes still darting back to the ring. "Did you know that she is the one who told me about that park?"

That caught his attention. "Really?"

"Yes!" She was indignant. "Just a few months before that horrible day. And today, she mentioned Esther's yellow jacket."

"Okay. Well, that was released with the alert." Billy frowned, not dismissing her, but not seeing a smoking gun.

"And her yellow boots."

He was now leaning forward making furious notes. Beth continued, "You didn't release that, and I had just purchased both items that day. There's no way she would have even known Esther had those boots." Beth didn't have to wait long for his response.

"I think I need to pay a visit to that office." He snapped the notebook closed.

"Billy there's something else. Can you tell me about the ring in that photograph?"

"I told you it was from one of the missing girls. She was wearing it the night she was abducted."

She got up and went to the kitchen, speaking as she left the room. "The other day, after Bible study," she began her confession. "It's actually been almost two weeks because it was just before…" She trailed off. Clearing her throat, she continued, "Melody shared a story about the abandoned movie theater over on Fifth. You know the one?"

He nodded his head.

"She had been through there a couple of times. Once she had seen a bus, then some old mattresses … so we drove over that afternoon."

He was ready to throttle her.

She held up her hands to calm him. "It was abandoned. There was no bus. No mattresses. The parking lot was empty. But we got out to look around the spot where Melody said the mattresses were—"

"Beth." Fear and anger caused his voice to rise. "That was beyond reckless. You know how dangerous that part of town is! Have you lost your mind?"

"Well, maybe a little. But I really thought Melody's imagination had just run wild. I mean, what are the odds of something so sinister going on *so close* to our neighborhood? Well, I know now." She fought the tears. "But I found this …" She laid the ring on the paperwork in front of her husband.

He looked at her, baffled. He picked the small band up and examined it closer. It had the same inscription. "You found this at the movie theater?"

"Yes," she stated simply. "If you think the cases are connected then maybe this will help us find our girl. You need to check out Dr. Clark."

Billy wasted no time in setting up a meeting with Dr. Morrison. Even though it was after hours, he was willing to oblige the detective with a search through Dr. Clark's office.

Billy met the taller man in the office parking lot that night at eight o'clock and shook hands with him. With his cardigan sweater and khaki pants, the doctor reminded Billy of his grandfather.

"As the owner of this practice, I can allow you to search through her office—desk, personal file cabinet, etcetera—but I do ask that you refrain from going into the patient files." He opened the outside door and stepped inside. The alarm warning sounded, and Dr. Morrison tapped the keypad, entering the code to turn it off.

"That's fine." Billy was focused and followed the physician down the hall of the office space. Arriving at her office, clearly marked by her nameplate, Billy waited while Dr. Morrison fit the master into the lock.

"Here we are," Dr. Morrison stated, stepping aside so the detective could conduct his search.

"Thank you." Billy didn't move for a moment, evaluating the space in its entirety. It was sparse, no pictures on her desk. No art on the walls. The bookshelf held only a few medical journals. "When did you say she started with your practice?"

"June of last year. I had some slight misgivings, but she is highly skilled."

"Why did you have misgivings?" Billy questioned.

"She's been through multiple practices in the last few years. I chalked it up to her moves, but it still raises a red flag. I like to give people a chance, so that's why I hired her."

"I see." Billy took a step toward the bookshelf. Copies of *The New England Journal of Medicine* and *JAMA* were on the shelves. "No pictures. Does she have family?"

"She is quite private. She also sees patients at the local homeless shelters. Pro bono. She is passionate about helping the less fortunate. But here, she comes in, sees patients, stays in her office, and leaves. She doesn't like anyone coming into her office and she doesn't really mingle with the patients or staff."

"Yet she seems to know whenever Beth and the girls are here?"

"Come again?" Morrison asked.

"Beth explained that every time she's come for an appointment, Dr. Clark approaches her in some way."

He watched the physician's reaction to this information. Morrison shifted to his right leg, his hand scratching his right temple. "I was not aware that it was every time."

Billy moved toward her desk. A cherry-finished executive desk with a large center drawer flanked by two smaller pencil drawers. Below them, two file drawers. Billy pulled out the center drawer. A couple of file folders, several pens, sticky note pads with various drug company names, and a prescription pad. He shut the drawer and pulled out the next one. A dictation machine on the right side. The left-side file drawer was locked.

He ran a finger over a small carving in the corner of the desk ... a snake eating its tail.

"Sorry, I don't have the key to her desk, just the office." Morrison shrugged. "I really need to be getting home, Detective."

"Yes, thank you for letting me in, Dr. Morrison." Billy shuffled through the drawers once more. Taking the file folders from the center drawer, he skimmed through the contents.

"If those are patient files—" Dr. Morrison started as a reminder.

"They don't seem to be. At least, this one is just a spreadsheet with some names and dates. Not sure if those are patients." He replaced the file. When he went to open the second one, several photos fell from it onto the desk.

Dr. Morrison came over to look. "What are those?" he asked, concern etched in his face.

"They seem to be photos of children. Are these patients of yours?" There were no names on any of them, but they were all labeled "Blue Eyes."

Dr. Morrison leafed through the images. "Yes, I believe these are all patients here. Some of these children are established with me."

"And they all have brown hair and blue eyes," Billy noted. *Just like Esther.* He sorted through the contents, praying and hoping not to find Esther's image among them. His heart jumped to his throat when he found the photo of his daughter and her bright smile. He turned the image slowly to Dr. Morrison.

"Yes, they do—Oh my!" Dr. Morrison exclaimed when he recognized Esther's face. "But what does it prove?"

"Nothing, but it does warrant a conversation."

Billy pulled out his phone and snapped a few photos before replacing the contents of the folder, returning them all to the drawer. He pulled the first file out and photographed the spreadsheet. He would cross-reference the names to see if any of the kids had gone missing.

Turning to Dr. Morrison, Billy pocketed his cell phone. "Thank you again, Doctor. I think I have what I came for. I'll be in touch." He followed the same path out of the building as Dr. Morrison followed. Billy sat in his car watching the doctor lock up after him. He planned on coming by tomorrow, once the office opened, to have a conversation with Dr. Harriet Clark.

Forty-Two

When Billy entered the office, Dr. Clark stood abruptly. Billy noted her edginess and how she quickly closed her center drawer.

"Good morning, Dr. Clark." Billy flashed his badge. "I'm Detective Everett."

"Oh yes, Beth's husband." Her eyes darted around the room as she spoke, reminding Billy of a caged animal.

"I wondered if I could ask you some questions," he started.

"Oh, so sorry, Detective. I make it a point not to speak with any authority without my lawyer's consent. I'm sure you understand. We live in such a litigious society." She rattled off her answer.

"I see." Billy stared at her long and hard.

She awkwardly sat back down at her desk.

"Yes, so, unless you were to arrest me for something … are you going to arrest me for something?" she asked, now holding his gaze. After a moment, she broke away, dismissing him while returning to her paperwork. "I have work to do, so if you don't mind." She pulled out her prescription pad and made herself busy writing a script.

Billy was not deterred. There was only one thing he needed to see. "No, I just wondered what 'Blue Eyes' might mean to you?"

His eyes narrowed as he watched her face pale, and the pen falter in her hand.

She coughed and cleared her throat. Never looking up, she simply replied, "Nothing. It means nothing to me."

Stacey Herring

Harriet entered the rectangle room as though she fancied herself the ruler of this sordid underworld. Her hair was frazzled, and she seemed a bit unsteady on her feet, apparently inebriated. The smell of alcohol followed her in. She searched the room, snarling when she saw Cassie, but moved on to the one she was seeking—Missy.

Cassie was not out of earshot as they spoke in hushed tones. Thanks to Ethan and his call with Harriet, Cassie was fully aware of their plan for her child. She listened intently in the hope of learning any details about when this event would occur and prayed desperately that God would intervene.

"Missy." Harriet placed a firm arm around the young girl's shoulder. "I have something to discuss with you."

Cassie shifted so she could best hear the conversation, pretending to be busy with Esther, Lily, and Anna. She saw with interest that Esther was watching Harriet, almost as if she recognized her but couldn't place from where. Something in Cassie told her to hide Esther. She moved her behind Lily and Anna. Cassie took in every bit of their discussion.

"Of course," Missy assured her, looking up shyly at the older woman. Cassie saw the brokenhearted girl eager for a mother's approval.

"We both know you should be the overseer here. Cassie"—she spat the name—"may have assumed the role, but I intend to change that."

Cassie didn't react to her name. She remained aloof as she braided Lily's hair.

Missy brightened and stood a little taller, her chin thrust forward. "That is exactly what I thought from the beginning. Thank you for seeing it too, Harriet. Whatever you can do, I would really be thankful."

"I am practically half owner of this business, and I will start using some of that authority. I am tired of the men making the decisions when they are so misguided." She grimaced and laughed a bit too loud, leaning in on Missy to keep her balance. Missy turned her head as the large woman breathed heavily in her face.

Harriet's whisper was loud and slurred. "You and I are a lot alike, Missy. You're strong and brave, and you know how to get what you want. How old are you?"

"Thirteen, ma'am," Missy replied obediently.

"Ah, yes. Thirteen. What a great age. I made some strong commitments at that age. Do you think you could make a commitment to me?"

"Yes, ma'am. I would, if you help me to get what I want," Missy countered.

A cunning grin broke across Harriet's face. "Yes, that's it. You always need to fight for what you want. Don't give anything away for free. I made a sacrifice when I was your age. It was my first one. I decided I knew what I wanted and wasn't going to wait on my repulsive uncle to bring it."

Missy hesitated. "What will I have to sacrifice?"

"Oh, nothing yet," Harriet cooed. "In due time, I will let you know. But for now, I need eyes in here. I need to have someone close to tell me what is going on. Someone on the inside that I can trust."

"But I thought you and Ethan were partners?" Missy's eyebrows pulled together, and she tilted her head slightly.

"Oh yes, but I don't *trust* him, Missy. He is out for himself, and he doesn't tell me everything. You see, he's threatened by me. So he keeps secrets. And now that cop is asking me things …" Missy nodded her head. "But you won't keep secrets from me, will you, Missy?"

"No, ma'am. I'll tell you what you want to know, but what will you do for me?" she asked, standing a little taller—now eye-to-eye with Harriet.

"Well, I'll make you the one in charge. You will get to decide who stays and who goes." She looked directly at Cassie. "You will be the one to recruit new kids and bring them into the family."

"Okay. I would like that." Missy paused. "I deserve that. It was easy bringing in that little brat."

The reference to Esther seemed to prod Harriet's mind, "Oh right. Where is that little girl?"

Esther peeked around Anna.

"Cassie took her." Missy's tone dripped with scorn. Harriet glared in Cassie's direction.

"What do you want to know?" Missy pressed.

Harriet turned her attention back to Missy. "Cassie is going to have a baby. She is only a couple of months away. I need to know when she goes into labor. I need you to watch her. And tell me anything interesting that goes on." She was rubbing Missy's shoulders now.

Missy's eyes narrowed; she shot a scathing look at Cassie.

Harriet wobbled a bit as she made her way across the room to Cassie. Missy followed with a new look of superiority in her eyes.

"I know you hear us, girl," Harriet declared, again her words slightly slurred. "Where is that little brat that we brought here? Where is Esther?"

Esther popped her head up at her name but moved closer to Cassie, "Dr. Clark?" she whispered, her brows pulled together in confusion.

Cassie ignored the drunken woman until she was looming over her. She slowly stood, her burgeoning belly making it more of a task each day. She looked Harriet in the eyes and asked, "What about Esther?"

Harriet bent down, leaning past Cassie's legs to get a glimpse of the child. "You. Your mom and dad. They are no good."

Cassie shifted to block Harriet with her body. Esther began to cry.

"I made a promise. I was made a promise," Harriet mumbled, nearly incoherently. She stood abruptly, and nearly fell into Missy. "I told him I would serve him if he made me wealthy and powerful. And I didn't want that horrible, wretched man touching me ever again. My uncle was scum." She looked up at Cassie, poking a finger at her chest. "You don't get to take it all away. We are going to use you to bring power to our spells. You, your baby"—here she pointed at Esther—"and that brat." She turned and leaned hard on Missy.

"Missy." Her face was inches from Missy's. "Tell me when she starts labor pains. Call me."

"I don't have a way to call you, Harriet." Missy coughed and turned her head away from Harriet's heavy breathing.

Harriet's face split into a stupid grin. She reached into the pocket of her flowing dress and produced a phone. An old model; Cassie could see it was a flip phone. Hope flashed before her. "You do now, Missy. You only call me—got it? And don't let any of these wretches take that phone. I can trust you, right, Missy?"

"Yes, ma'am," Missy assured her. "No one will touch this phone." She dared everyone with a glare.

"Good." Harriet patted her cheek. "Good girl."

Harriet turned to leave, not letting go of Missy. The two walked together to the door as Amber entered.

"What's going on?" Amber questioned Harriet, ignoring Missy.

"Missy will take charge over Cassie. She will be her overseer to report when her labor begins." Harriet patted Missy on the shoulders. Cassie held her breath.

"Ethan said he wanted me to—" Amber sounded unsure.

"Oh, surely you have more important things to do than babysit. And when Ethan and I spoke, we agreed to Missy since she is already here. I'll talk with Ethan and straighten it all out." With a withering glance back at Cassie, Harriet left the room.

Amber shrugged. "Whatever."

Cassie watched them, still standing, ready to fight if she had to. *Lord, the time is coming. You will need to move. Soon. Very soon.* She felt the baby flutter inside of her, and she rubbed the spot where he moved.

No one is getting this baby or this little girl. I'll die protecting them.

Forty-Three

Beth and Melody were sipping coffee while waiting for Mae. Both, burdened by the heaviness of all they were going through, had been sitting in silence. Beth was exhausted after searching the park and surrounding areas again, hoping for any clue that might lead to her child. The police led the manhunt, but Beth needed to feel like an active participant. She had spent the better part of the day searching, with Maggie close at hand.

Now Maggie napped on the couch in Melody's living room.

Mae bustled in, late as usual. This time, she held a tray of brownies along with her canvas tote, her Bible, and her purse. She laid the brownies down on the kitchen counter, hung the tote over her chair, and set her Bible on the table and her purse next to it.

"Oh, what a week!" She huffed as she flopped down onto the chair. "Is there any news, Beth?"

Melody sat at the head of the table and Beth on her right. Mae settled into the seat on Melody's left.

Beth shook her head in answer to Mae's question. "No, they've made no headway. How can a child just disappear like that? What kind of system must be in place? I've gone myself every day, starting at the park and knocking on businesses and homes for blocks. No one recognizes Esther." She drew her arms around her body.

"I'm so sorry, dear." She paused, then turned to Melody, patting her forearm. "How are you healing, Melody?"

Fields of Gomorrah

She shrugged. "Every day is better. The fear is subsiding. I went to the grocery store by myself for the first time this week. It is just horrible to feel so weak and vulnerable."

"I've been doing some research into the fields in your dreams, Beth." Mae pulled out her notebook from the canvas tote. She licked her finger and turned several pages.

Beth was interested in what she might have found. She leaned toward her friend and asked her to share.

"Here it is. Okay, so in the Bible a field represented a promise. Think of Ruth and Boaz."

"But my field was all death and darkness."

"Yes, I considered that. That made me think of the scripture in Deuteronomy. We're nearly to it in our monthly study, actually. In chapter 32, Moses is giving one of his final speeches. Verses 9 through 12 talk about God's children: 'For the LORD's portion is his people; Jacob is the lot of his inheritance. He found him in a desert land, and in the waste howling wilderness.' That sounds a bit like your field, yes?"

Beth nodded in agreement.

Mae continued reading. "He led him about, he instructed him, he kept him as the apple of his eye. As an eagle stirs up her nest, flutters over her young, spreads abroad her wings, takes them, bears them on her wings: so the LORD alone did lead him, and there was no strange god with him."

Mae looked across to Beth and held her eyes. "I have faith that Esther is alive," she said.

A broken sob escaped from Beth. Melody placed an arm around her shoulder.

Mae looked at her softly. "I believe wherever she is, the Lord is keeping watch over her. Let me read a bit further." She mumbled through a few verses. "Talks about how the children of Israel went astray ... took other gods ... Oh yes, here, verses 31, 32, and 35: 'For their rock is not as our Rock, even our enemies themselves being judges.' So, you see here"—Mae looked from one to the other, and Beth gave her an encouraging nod—"God is established. He is our Rock. The one that our enemies work for is not like our God. And they know it. 'For their vine is the vine of Sodom, and of the fields of Gomorrah: their grapes are grapes of gall, their clusters are bitter.'"

Beth considered what Mae read and chimed in, "There is 'field' again. And how barren and fallow would the fields of Gomorrah be?"

Mae smiled, "They would surely be an uncultivated wasteland! But listen here, verse 35: 'To me belongs vengeance and recompence; their foot shall slide in due time: for the day of their calamity is at hand, and the things that shall come upon them make haste.' I think this trial will come to an end soon. I believe that God is fighting for us. We need only be still."

Beth shuddered, wiping fresh tears from her eyes. "That is good news, Mae. Because I think that is all I am capable of doing. I pray you are right."

Forty-four

Melody picked up the phone on the third ring. She pulled the receiver from her ear at the high-pitched panic of Mae at the other end of the line.

"Mae?" Melody raised her voice to speak over the agitated woman. "Mae, please. I can't understand you. Is everything okay? What's wrong?" An unease began to grow in Melody's spirit. She whispered, "Lord Jesus, what could be wrong?"

"Melody." Mae was finally calming down to a coherent level. "A young girl came into the office. Flanked by Ethan's men. Why would a sixteen-year-old need to be escorted? No good. No good. He said it is part of his Homeless Humanity project." She huffed. "But that man was here again, Draven Wolfe." She spat the name out with contempt. "I know it was him, but Ethan won't discuss it. And again, he was here, stormed in like he owned the company instead of Ethan. Oh Lord, have mercy. I know I wasn't meant to see them. I barely made it to my desk when Draven left. About an hour later, I saw Ethan leave with the girl." She inhaled deeply.

"He seemed so broken. I'm so worried about him. He slipped out the back too. Which is not unusual for him. But walking out without his briefcase—now that is unusual. He was never more than three feet away from that case. And to leave for the day, without it? Well, I never saw that.

"So after he left ..." She paused.

Melody was eager to know what happened. "Mae, after he left. What happened?"

"Well," she began slowly. "Okay so, I went into the office. I had to, of course, to make sure the lights were out. Yes." She seemed to be convincing herself of the fact more than Melody. "Yes, yes, of course. I always check his office before I leave for the day. Nothing wrong with that. It's just my routine, that's what. And I noticed his planner was almost open on his desk."

Melody risked an interruption. "What do you mean, almost open?"

Mae stammered a little, "W-well, you know. It was on his desk. And when I walked over to tidy up, it sort of fell open."

Melody let it slide. *Lord, she needs a dozen angels!* "And what did you see, Mae?" she pressed.

"Something about an appointment in that plaza over on Tenth Avenue on the twentieth. You know, with the pizza place and that fish market. Okay, fine. That's fine. But then I saw the time. Midnight. Why would he have a meeting at midnight? Highly suspect, I tell you, Melody. Something is wrong. Something horrible is going to happen. I just have the Holy Ghost feeling. So of course I had to call you. To tell you—and maybe your police friend should know. And, oh, I don't know. Stake out the joint or something."

"Yeah, you're probably right. I'll call and speak with Beth."

"Oh, and Melody—one more thing. The girl." Mae paused.

"Yes?"

"She was pregnant." Mae sounded broken.

"Trafficked." Melody breathed the word with heaviness of heart.

"I do believe so," Mae agreed. "The CEO of a corporation doesn't just bring in a pregnant teenager he finds on the street."

"Oh, Mae. God is moving."

The women prayed together before ending the call.

After the call, Melody pulled out her notebook. There was a nagging thought that she could not place or let go of. Something that Mae had said stuck in Melody's mind. Leafing through her prayer journal, she found the page of notes she had compiled over the last few months. Reviewing the list of words, she had received in her prayer time, she froze, nearly falling off the couch. Her eyes stopped at one of the phrases that was so random, she had dismissed it: "At the fish." There, written by her own hand, were words that could only be connected to this meeting Ethan was to have in less than two weeks at the fish market on Tenth Avenue.

Her eyes skimmed to the date she had written it down. September 20. She sat in awe of God for nearly ten minutes before dialing Beth on the phone. Billy should know about this. And a stakeout was surely in order.

Forty-Five

It was late. Cold pizza sat on the countertop, and Maggie was passed out on the living room couch as a movie with dancing cartoons streamed on the TV. The Everetts and Reys and their pastor, Carl Smith, were gathered in the kitchen.

"It just can't be a coincidence, Billy," Melody said. "That I would get a word meaning 'at the fish,' and Ethan has a meeting at the fish market? It was such a random word; I had dismissed it as something of my own making. But now it seems to mean something."

Billy shook his head. He couldn't wrap his mind around this yet. He had been back to the office since the day the chief had sent him home, but he always felt the wary eye of his overseer on him. He certainly couldn't go in and say his wife's friend had a premonition, but the meeting was something he could work with. He and Beth had asked everyone over for dinner so they could discuss these details and, more importantly, spend some time in prayer.

"So if I piece this together correctly," said the pastor, "this all began with a dream that Beth had?" He shook his head in amazement. "Amazing."

The couples turned expectant eyes to their spiritual leader for guidance. They were all out of their depth and were eager for some direction.

Billy said, "But what do we do with this? I know we wrestle against spiritual wickedness in high places. But this is a flesh-and-blood business. Quite literally. And our daughter is apparently caught up in it. We have no idea what this midnight meeting could be about. And how does it all tie into the abducted children? How can I battle something that I have no power to move on?" His exasperation soaked every word as the burden of his daughter, Cassie, and countless innocents weighed on his heart and mind.

Pastor Carl cleared his throat to speak, but Melody started before him. "I think I know the significance of the date, but the location is a mystery to me. The twentieth is the summer solstice." She spoke quietly. "That is a holy day for satanic cults. And a blood …" Her voice broke. She turned watery eyes toward Beth. "I don't think it was just a dream, Beth."

Beth gasped and turned wild eyes to her husband.

He took her hand, unable to speak for a moment.

Carl picked up for Melody. "Yes, a blood sacrifice. The Brotherhood of the White Temple has long been known to exist here in our city." He stood and walked to the sink to rinse his coffee mug. Clearly, having something to do gave him a moment to process. His back was to them for a moment. "We really must pray," he said, mostly to himself.

Then he turned to address the group. "You're right, Billy. It is a spiritual battle, and we need to allow God to fight it. But there will be action required on our part. We need to go into this battle together and ready."

He turned from the sink and looked at the four weary warriors seated at the humble kitchen table. He spoke with confidence. "I don't think we are ever really prepared for this. Your child is missing. Melody was physically attacked. The battle is real."

His smile encouraged them. "However, we can do this. Jesus is equipping us with every step of faith we take. He is here, in our midst, even now." He held up his hands up in front of his chest as he spoke. "We often tend to think of God versus Satan, right?"

Billy nodded with the others.

Pastor Carl continued, "God and Satan. But! It's actually, God"—he lowered his left hand, while his right hand remained at chest height—"and Satan. God created Satan. They are not equals. It is our God who is all-powerful. Satan only wishes he were. He mimics and mocks God, but his power is limited. And as his nature warrants, he lies to his followers that he is as powerful as God. The enemy convinces many that he has power, and indeed it can seem that way. But he mostly has tricks. He is the father of lies, and since he has been around so long, he understands how the human mind works and our three areas of weakness—lust of the eye, lust of the flesh, and the pride of life. He uses these three weaknesses to his advantage daily. But that is not power, per se."

Billy was still unsatisfied. "Pastor, I don't think I've conveyed the enormity of this situation to you. I am nearly off this case. I am being watched closely. All signs point to my own daughter being one of the victims! Why would God provide this insight, knowing we are powerless to stop it? Why on earth did He allow this to happen in the first place?" His voice broke. He cleared his throat, running hands through his hair in his frustration, as the deeper pain and confusion was revealed.

Carl's face was filled with compassion. He walked to Billy and placed a hand on his shoulder. "There are times in our lives when we question why such a good, kind, loving Father would allow such grievous pain into the lives of His creation. The answer does not satisfy our human mind. We live in a fallen world, yes. Satan has some authority in this world, but God is still the ultimate authority. Still, none of these words ease the pain of the reality that evil brings. They don't bring your child home. Words alone do not suffice in explaining why these children were left in the darkness of this world to be preyed on again and again."

"Exactly," Billy agreed.

Carl began to pray in the Spirit, asking for intercession and healing. Beseeching the Lord to blanket them in His love and to bolster their faith. Keeping a hand on Billy's shoulder, he lifted the other to Beth's. In turn, Beth grabbed Melody's hand, as she held Scott's. The circle was completed when Scott placed his hand on Billy's shoulder. Together, they marched into the spiritual battle.

As they prayed, Billy felt a new boldness. A plan was beginning to form in his mind. Promises filled his thoughts: The children would be saved. Esther would be found, along with Cassie and Lily and many more. The children would be freed, returned to their homes, and one day used for even greater things.

The Spirit flooded the room, tears flowed, and prayers were lifted. He had never felt God's presence so intensely. It reaffirmed that everything they faced, this baseless evil, was part of their destiny to destroy.

Strongholds were falling as they prayed.

Forty-Six

Cassie felt the first contraction that morning. Afraid to allow Missy to see the pain, she turned to the wall and began to pray.

Esther placed a soft hand on her shoulder. "Are you okay, Miss Cassie?"

"Yes," she whispered, her breath ragged. "I will be okay."

She held back a cry as the pain took her. She had worked so hard to keep Esther protected. No one had taken her in the time she'd been there. She was scared, but untouched. Cassie now suspected that the guards had reserved her for this horrible night's events. *Maybe God will ...* The next wave of pain engulfed her.

The pangs intensified over the course of the day. By evening, Cassie's body could no longer hide the truth.

Missy noticed something was amiss and came close to Cassie. "It begins" was all she said as she once again retreated. Cassie turned her prayers to Missy.

"Stop it." She hissed through closed teeth. "Stop praying for Missy. She is ours."

This time, Cassie didn't stop, she was emboldened. With nothing left to risk, and everything to lose, she pressed on. "I won't stop," she said with more courage than she knew she had. "I'll keep praying for her to be free of you, in Jesus's name."

Missy lurched backward against the wall at the name. She bared her teeth like a caged animal. Her nails scraped against the steel, and she continued to hiss, guttural sounds coming from deep within her.

"She wants us," the voice declared. "She asked us in."

"Maybe she doesn't want you anymore!" Cassie declared. "Missy, do you want them?"

The internal battle was visible as Missy's head was saying no. Her mouth moved as if to speak, yet no words came through.

Deciding to equip her with knowledge that would be up to her to use, she spoke quickly, "Missy, you only have …" Before she could say more, another wave of pangs encompassed her. She gasped out the truth as strongly as she could. "You only have to ask—" she winced, taking short breaths.

"No!" The demons howled and shrieked with Missy's voice. "Don't say His name. Don't speak it to us!"

"You only have to ask Jesus to come in." Her hand digging into her thigh, she breathed through the pain of the contraction. Looking up, she saw Missy, scared and alone, but only for a moment, and she was gone again. Steely eyes glared back at Cassie.

"The baby comes. You cannot stop what will happen." The demon within Missy began singing in its excitement. "It comes! The sacrifice!"

"Never! You will not sacrifice my baby! *In Jesus's name!*"

They screamed, a legion of voices coming as a multitude, and she covered her ears. The children whimpered, and Esther drew closer to her. Already tucked in the corner of the room, they recoiled at the sound, huddling together. Terror sliced through Cassie's heart as she cried out to God.

Missy stormed over to the group and began kicking Cassie repeatedly. Cassie realized Missy was gone; her mind taken over. The gleeful howl that burst from her wide-open mouth as she kicked Cassie's swollen abdomen was inhuman. Curling into the fetal position, she protected the baby as best she could as the children scattered. The kicks rained down. Missy was uncontrollable. *They* were uncontrollable.

Apparently hearing the commotion, the guards rushed in. Their voices added to the chaos as they shouted their commands. The terrified children cried out in fear and confusion.

"Get Missy!" Amber yelled to Melvin, pointing at the lunatic.

Melvin ran to Missy and pulled her off of Cassie. Her body thrashed against the guard as she lurched to reach Cassie once more. Amber arrived at Cassie's side and assessed the damage.

"She's a bloody mess. What the …" She cursed. She stood and marched over to Missy. "What were you thinking? She's the sacrifice, you fool!" She smacked her hard across the face.

Missy's lip split, and she smiled as blood trickled from her mouth. Amber shivered and turned back to Cassie. Missy broke free of Melvin and jumped onto Amber's back, biting her ear and tearing at her face with her sharp fingernails.

Amber screamed as Melvin grappled to remove the rabid child. Dropping to her back, Amber knocked the wind briefly out of Missy as she collided with the steel floor. Melvin had her on her stomach in a flash, pulling her arms tight across her back. He grabbed zip ties from his pocket and secured them with what looked to be exceptional force. Missy cried out in pain. Both guards ignored it.

"Keep her away from Cassie, and call the doctor!" Amber demanded, holding her ear.

The guard returned to check on Cassie. Panicking as she lifted a bloody hand to her face, Cassie was terrified for her baby. Her entire body throbbed, and she felt a new pang. Crying and scared, she listened to the guards' exchange.

"What happened?" Hector demanded an explanation from the other guards, having entered only after the havoc had ended. "She was to be protected. The child is intended for the master. Now what? Draven will be furious, and I'll make sure he knows who was in charge of this!"

"She went crazy, man! It was Clark that assigned the psycho to her. We were advised to give her free access. How would we know she would lose it, man?" Amber was furious, now tending to the scratches on her face and trying to get her ear to stop bleeding.

Fields of Gomorrah

"Well, it's done now. Call the doc. She will have to fix her own mistake. She is able to stop this. It's too soon." He looked back at Cassie as if she was a pathetic dog about to give birth to a litter of mongrels.

Turning her face to the wall, she prayed. *Lord, everything is surreal now. I feel like I'm floating through this reality. Am I about to give birth to my first child? My mother is not with me. She doesn't even know where I am, let alone that I'm pregnant. Oh, Jesus. What will happen now?*

She sobbed into the cold steel floor, which offered more comfort than the guards.

"Well, shut up now. The doc is on her way. She'll fix this." Hector was assuring himself. Nothing could fix this for Cassie.

Missy sat against the far wall. Her eyes never leaving Cassie. Her hair fell haphazardly across her face, and her hands were still tied. But the smile. Cassie shivered.

The children slowly made their way back to Cassie's side. She found great strength in their encouraging words and soft touch. Esther pulled the hair from Cassie's face. Timothy gently rubbed her arm while Lily and Anna softly sang to her the song she had taught them.

Soon, Harriet bustled through the door, yelling at the guards as she barged in. She carried a medical bag with her. Although the children recoiled at her voice, they did not leave Cassie.

"Let me see, you idiots. What happened? She just started kicking her? Oh, this is just great." Harriet looked briefly at Missy and dismissed the girl for a moment.

She kneeled beside Cassie, who pulled back in disgust. Missy's cohort. Anna's handler. Harriet was unfazed. She turned her attention to the children around Cassie, then focused on Esther alone.

"Blue Eyes," Harriet whispered, as she reached for Esther.

Cassie blocked her touch.

Harriet's steely gaze locked on Cassie. "Listen, I'm here to help." She sounded convincing. "I'm a pediatrician. You didn't know that, but I know how to make the bleeding stop and help you. Stop moving so I can do my job."

Cassie didn't trust her, and she didn't believe she wanted to actually help her, but she was assured that she could help the baby, and at least that would buy some more time. If the baby came now, there was nothing Cassie could do to change their fate. So she obeyed.

Harriet brought the medical bag close and began to pull out different items. A needle, an IV bag, and a vial with clear fluid. Harriet muttered something about telling him to set up a bed.

Turning to Cassie, as though she was part of her internal conversation, and an actual patient, she spoke with a pleasant bedside manner. "At least I had the foresight to be prepared. You never know how a birth is going to go, after all. We don't need it to arrive quite yet, but this should do the job." She smiled.

Cassie whimpered.

Harriet did indeed seem to be prepared with a myriad of medical necessities. Melvin came in with an IV stand, and she began to set it up. Cassie presumed it had been in the good doctor's car. The needle had been implanted in her flesh now, and the fluids were running through her veins. Harriet added something to the drip, and after a look around, she got up to leave.

"You must eat what they bring you," she counseled Cassie in that same doctor-patient voice. "You need to keep up your strength."

She walked over to Missy, and the child struggled to stand before her mentor.

"What do you think you were doing?" Harriet's tone could have skinned a cat.

"What I wanted," Missy declared; her chin jutted forward.

Harriet met the insolence with a hard blow across the face. "You will deal with the consequences then."

Cassie took in the sight. *Make a deal with the devil, and expect her to behave.*

Harriet turned to leave. She was decidedly stricter in her tone to the guards.

"I will be speaking with Draven about this incident. You know what she means for the summer solstice. You idiots have one job; to keep her safe and calm so the child is born without imperfection. Do you think you can manage this for the next forty-eight hours?"

While she did not try to disclose anything from Cassie, she had just given up the timeline. Cassie was drifting quickly, thanks to whatever Harriet had added to the IV. But in her last moments before fading, she went to the Lord to seek Him once more.

God had forty-eight hours to free them. There was some comfort in knowing He had a deadline.

Cassie awoke to a conspiracy of whispers. The children were huddled around her. As her blurry eyes came into focus, she recognized the item Timothy held. Missy's phone.

"How did you—" she stammered.

Timothy thrust the item toward her, unsure what to do and terrified of being caught. "We distracted her, and Lily grabbed it. She had left it in the corner. We saw the opportunity. She's been weird since the doctor left. Like a zombie."

Cassie sat up slowly, the pain raking over her body. "Okay, one call, and then we must put it back. The guards can't know we had it. Missy can't know."

She had tucked the card from the cop into her Bible but had committed the number to memory. After the third ring, it went to voicemail.

"Officer, um … Billy? It's Cassie. Cassie Woods …" She fumbled through the message. "I think we only have two days. The baby is due. They stopped the contractions, but the fat lady I told you about—she said she's a pediatrician—she said they have forty-eight hours before they need us. Please help us, Billy. They brought a new child in. Esther. She's so little.

Please save us! You can't call me back." She wiped the tears away and flipped the phone shut. She handed it back to Timothy. They shared the plan with Cassie of returning the phone.

Timothy, Lily, and Anna walked toward the Porta Potty. Acting nonchalantly, the plan was to draw Missy's attention to the girls. Lily slipped inside the blue booth while Anna stood at the door and Timothy moved in the shadows, placing the phone back where Missy had left it. Missy did not react—successful operation.

I should have erased the number, Cassie thought as anxiety took hold.

Forty-Seven

Billy finished playing the message for Chief Stone and the Feds. He had received it last night and called an emergency meeting for that morning. Dixon was there, and then he wasn't. Billy didn't notice when he had slipped out. He continued with the details he had learned from Dr. Clark's office and their conversation.

"She fits the case perfectly. She had access to my daughter. She knew what she was wearing—details we did not release. Cassie describes her as fat and just confirmed she's a pediatrician."

"Definitely, we need to put a detail on her." Chief Stone was grim. "We have two days to determine where they're going and what they're up to."

"I do have another detail on that. Long story, but a friend of my wife's took a job as the secretary for Ethan Walker several months ago. She's better than most detectives because she discovered that he has a midnight meeting on the twentieth."

Amir slapped a hand on the desk, the most reaction Billy had seen from him. "Two days from now!"

"Exactly," Billy said. "The address is vague, Tenth Avenue, but that is the plaza where the Wisdom Foundation is located."

Billy's heart was beating rapidly. Not only had they finally secured some leads, but the connections came in rapid-fire succession. First Dr. Clark slipping up on the unreleased detail, Ethan's meeting, and now Cassie tying it all in together.

Amir tapped his fingers against the desk. "But where does Draven come in?"

"I'm not sure yet, but I am pretty confident we can ask him ourselves in two days. My gut says this is the only reason he is involved with Ethan. It's the perfect front for him because it's owned by someone else. Ethan is a fall guy, whether he knows it or not."

Chief Stone sat back in his chair. His face solemn. "Billy, I can't have you on this case." Billy erupted in angry disagreement. Stone raised a hand to silence him. "You are too close. You have done excellent work here. Let us take it from here. We will get your daughter back. You need to rest."

Billy stormed out of the office and through the front door. There was no way he could rest until his daughter was found.

Forty-Eight

James came in the next morning while Harriet was removing the IV from Cassie's arm. Cassie was almost glad to see him. The expression on his face told her it was not good.

He was slobbering and couldn't catch his breath as he approached Cassie. "Ethan couldn't fix it."

Her heart sank and fear flooded in. Her opportunities were slamming shut. She saw no way out.

"I told you the plan was set, Cassie. Where is your God now?" Harriet seemed to be looking at something in the shadow. "What … what is that?" She looked at Cassie and marched over to the corner.

Cassie objected, "No! It's mine."

With the Bible in her hands, Harriet snorted. "You have nothing," she sneered. Turning the book over in her hands, she scoffed, "A Bible? How did you get this?"

Cassie refused to answer, but James babbled on, "I gave it to her. It was a gift. Cassie likes the Bible." James nodded emphatically, patting the top of Cassie's head as if she was a loyal hound. Cassie's shoulders slumped, and she prayed the woman wouldn't open it.

Those prayers were answered, at least for now. Harriet took the book with her, but the disdainful look on her face gave Cassie peace that she would have no desire to read any part of it. Still, when Harriet left with Cassie's Bible, her loneliness intensified.

The door screeched open, and Draven and Ethan stepped in. Draven carried a small black briefcase.

Cassie was relieved that Harriet had already left with the Bible. Draven walked over to Cassie and placed his hand on her burgeoning belly. She recoiled. James defiantly stepped in front of her, knocking the man's hand away.

Draven smiled, placing the briefcase down on the floor. Not a good smile. The evil in his expression caused an ice-cold blast to trickle down Cassie's spine.

"James, I find it very convenient that you are here. There is a matter I need to settle with you."

James stood in confusion. Standing near the entrance, Ethan sprang into action, coming over to the three of them.

"Leave him be, Draven."

"I ... I don't want any trouble, Mr. Wolfe. I'm sorry I did that. It's just ..." James hesitated briefly then, catching Ethan's eye, he plowed ahead. "It's my baby, you see."

Ethan interjected, "James. Be quiet."

Draven waved him off with a flick of his hand, seeming to infuriate Ethan even more. "James. I had an interesting conversation with my contact at the police station."

James's face lost all color.

"Oh, so we do understand, do we?"

Ethan tried to stand between the two men, but James was frantic. He was pacing the floor in wide circles. The children scooted out of his way so not to be stepped on.

"Listen here, Draven. I deal with my brother," Ethan demanded. "Nobody else. Do you understand?"

"Do you realize what he's done, Ethan? It can't be good for your business, and it is certainly not good for mine. He made a trip to the police. Didn't you, James?"

James was crying and shaking his head. Cassie stood frozen in horror, forced to witness this tragedy unfold.

In a swift move, Draven pulled a pistol from his briefcase.

"I ... I didn't m-mean to, Ethan." James stammered as he looked at his brother for help.

"Told them to check out the shipping containers." Draven's eyes narrowed and his voice grew darker. "Nobody sells me out, Ethan. Nobody has a change of heart when working with me. Not you. And not him."

Draven looked at Ethan directly when he spoke the last words. Then he leveled the gun at James and fired. Ethan screamed out a final warning. But it was too late. The sound of the gun echoed off the walls, and the children wailed in fear causing chaos in the room. Cassie shrieked as she watched James fall to the floor and blood pool around him. The children sat in shock and an eerie silence broken only by James's whimpering.

Ethan rushed to his brother, his face pale and his eyes brimming with tears. Ethan held his brother's head in his lap. Cassie thought of what he had shared with her—the memory of holding his mother as she died and now his brother.

Draven looked down at the pair and laughed. Before leaving the room, he bent over Cassie's shoulder and whispered in her ear, "There now, I took care of the issue, dear. I will see you again soon."

She pulled back from his touch, unable to avoid the rank breath that circled around her face and crept into her nostrils. His eyes were cold as stone. In that moment, she witnessed true evil.

"I'm sorry, James. I'm so sorry." Ethan whispered all the promises he had made when they were children. "It was my job to protect you. It was my job ... I promised her."

James lifted a bloodied hand to Ethan, placing it on the side of his face. Tears mingled with blood as Ethan held fast to his brother. "It's okay, brother. You always took good care of me. You are good, Ethan." He faded from this world as Ethan wept, holding his lifeless body in his lap.

Moments passed. Cassie was stunned, staring into nothing, completely frozen.

After setting his brother's head on the floor, Ethan pulled out his phone. A single call set a flurry of activity in motion as the guards hurried in and removed the body.

Ethan sat silently, staring into space. Mumbling to himself about his brother, Draven, revenge … He slowly registered Cassie's presence.

"And you … pregnant with his child." Cassie didn't hear anger in his tone—regret maybe. "That child is the only family I have left. How can I allow this?" he asked out loud.

Forty-Nine

Two days had ticked by, and Cassie's hope dwindled that the cop would save them or that Ethan had any power to stop it. She knew from the smile on Missy's face that this would be the final meal. Her sinister laugh as she whispered details of what they were going to do echoed in her mind.

"They'll cut the child from you." She was gleeful. "Sacrifice it to the master. You watch and see."

Cassie knew now that the moment had come, and time had run out. Missy mocked her, but she no longer influenced her.

She finished the meal without incident. Although uncomfortable with the way Missy watched her as she ate, Cassie remained oddly calm.

Cassie didn't fight the guards this time. Missy wanted her to, practically begged her to. Whatever punishment she had received had settled in enough to prevent her from touching Cassie again. But Cassie had no fight left, and now as she was led from the room, her thoughts were of the children she was leaving behind. No one was left to protect them. To pray over them. To hold them after …

She thought of her unborn baby. The child he or she could have been … should have been. And she walked beside the guards, praying for an army of angels to descend. But nothing. She looked back once at the children. Dirty and worn, their tear-stained faces were more than she could bear. *Oh Lord, hear my cry!*

She was loaded into another SUV. They lifted the back hatch and Missy climbed in. Moments later, Melvin carried Esther over his shoulder and tossed her into the backseat next to Cassie. Cassie automatically drew Esther close, pushing away the thoughts of why they were bringing her too. *Surely two lives are enough!* Fury filled her mind.

"Why the kid?" Amber asked Melvin.

Melvin shrugged, "Harriet said something about insurance. Said make sure we brought her. She's untouched, you know, so maybe part of the ceremony. I have no idea what that woman rambles on about."

Cassie gasped softly and tightened her grip on Esther, never feeling more powerless than at that moment.

They drove along a myriad of city streets. Cassie didn't bother counting. They didn't bother with the blindfold. Everyone knew the girls weren't going to return. Esther nestled herself under Cassie's arm. The streetlights flashed in the windows. At the strip mall, Cassie took in the surroundings. A pizza shop, the Wisdom Foundation, a market. All so average—so unassuming. It was a strip mall like countless others, a place she and her mother would go to get their nails done, pick up dinner, grab a coffee.

Mom. Dad. I really won't see them again? This is the end of my story. My life? It isn't just another chapter. And Esther—Oh God, You must protect her!

She was numb now. Tears no longer fell. There was nothing left to give. She was empty.

Fifty

Exiting the van, Esther became Cassie's shadow. Struck by the fear in her eyes, Cassie wished there was something she could do. But only God could save them now.

They walked through the back alley that led to a loading dock. Climbing the cement steps, Cassie paused as a new pang washed over her. The uncaring guards pushed them through the double doors.

"Keep moving," Amber demanded gruffly. Their anticipation was palpable. She knew the plan. Missy had shared it to torture her. Still, she had no fight. She had no tears. She just whispered one name: "Jesus." She felt Esther's small hand in hers.

Prodding them along, Hector and Melvin directed them to a large walk-in freezer. The smell of dead fish assaulted her senses as cold seeped into her bones. Esther and Cassie huddled close together. Cassie was thankful that Esther still wore her little yellow jacket. The numbing of her heart began to give way to new fear as the enormity of the situation sank in. Cassie shivered as the cold seized her body. She felt a contraction coming.

Esther screamed as Amber wrestled her from the room.

Dragging her away from Esther, they yanked Cassie's arms over her head and zip-tied them to a chain. "No! Esther! Leave her alone!" Cassie cried out against the torment and the pain. Moaning from the agony in her abdomen, she braced herself against throbbing in her arms as they revolted against the pressure of the ties. Her body convulsed. Her baby was coming.

Tormented by all the things Missy had whispered, her heart sank.

Harriet arrived, dressed in a long black robe, the hood draped down her back. She wheeled in a tray with several knives and other instruments. Cassie groaned. Harriet's smile was hungry, yet slow disappointment spread across her face.

"There's no need to cut her," she said grimly. "The baby is coming already. You fools waited too long. It won't be long. I need to get one more thing." She looked at the guards. "You can go next door. The ceremony will begin soon. She's not going anywhere." Harriet laughed as she hurried from the room, picking up her flowing robe so she could be quick.

Missy slipped into the room and stood before Cassie. She was at war again. Missy. Renata. She struggled to be free.

"Where is Esther?" Cassie demanded.

Missy's eyes filled with tears. "I don't want to do this."

"Hide her then, from these murderers," Cassie pleaded.

Missy nodded. "I will." She ran from the room.

Harriet returned to the room, the small Bible now lying on the tray of instruments. Cassie screamed as the baby left her body. Harriet was ready and now wrapped the child in a blanket as she smacked it until it cried.

"Draven will be pleased," Harriet assured her. "A boy."

She held him up for Cassie to see, probably thinking it would tear her apart. Instead, it bolstered what tiny spark of hope she had left. *Surely Jesus will save him!*

Emotions on overload, her body exhausted, her mind numbed, seeing Harriet standing there, holding the baby, emptiness filled Cassie. She had failed. Unable to protect any of them, she had saved none of them. The last year of hell had been for nothing. She existed only to die. And now she was ready to do just that.

"Oh, and look!" Harriet shifted the child to one arm as she grabbed the Bible. "I also brought this to add to tonight's ritual! You brought so much to this offering, Cassie. Thank you."

As the baby left the room with Harriet, all her hope went with him. She felt the darkness call her, and her eyes grew heavy.

Fifty-One

Cassie looked up, confused and surprised, at the man standing before her. She had lost a lot of blood and her body was weak. She wondered if she was dreaming. "Ethan?" she asked, confused.

"Cassie. I—" He stumbled, cutting her free of the ties that bound her. "I never intended to be caught up in all of this. I can't make it right, but I can try to stop it." He laid her gently on the floor.

She looked up through a haze, her peripheral vision fuzzy. She felt tethered to her body. Not quite in it. "The baby. Esther. Save them." Her head lobbed to the side.

Billy was the first to arrive at the Wisdom Foundation around six o'clock. He had decided against telling Dixon the plan. The man had been erratic, and with his new tattoo, Billy believed he knew where Dixon's loyalties lay. He knew he was disobeying direct orders, but he didn't care. All that mattered was getting Esther back. He knew the others were scheduled to arrive low profile around eleven thirty.

He had parked on the far end of the L-shaped plaza and walked the entire site. He kept his hoodie up when he got close to the Wisdom Foundation. If they had cameras, he didn't want to raise any questions. *Just a guy walking by.*

Two broad windows spanned the front of the brick wall, flanking the door. The Wisdom Foundation logo was emblazoned across both panes. The windows were blackened and prevented Billy from seeing in.

Around back, he found no surprises. Back doors, garbage bins, and trash littering the roadway. A single-pane door offered him an awkward angle of space. He peered inside. It seemed to open to a small office. Nothing showed any signs of life within the foundation.

The shops were closed or closing for the day. The team in place the last two days reported that these regular workers were apparently unaware of the dark happenings of the Wisdom Foundation. Billy grabbed some dinner and returned to his car to eat.

The two men on Dr. Clark's detail had radioed in that she was on her way around ten thirty. Billy's wrapped food sat untouched in the white paper bag. He tried to stay focused on the job, but the thought that he might find his daughter tonight kept playing out in his mind.

Thirty minutes later, Billy saw a black SUV arrive and drive to the back alley. His heart beat rapidly. *It all comes together tonight, Lord. Watch over us.* Surely the rest of the team would be arriving soon.

He slipped from his car and blended in with the shadows of the night. Cutting into the back of the building, five shops before the Foundation, he crouched down and looked down the alley through night vision binoculars. He saw three heavily armed guards and three children. His heart was in his throat when he saw Esther in her yellow jacket. He forced himself to remain hidden. It took all of his strength. *God, protect her. Keep me sharp. Backup is coming in less than thirty minutes.*

He deftly moved through the back alley, now empty, and flattened himself against the brick exterior. He peered in the small window; the room was empty. Finding the door unlocked, he slipped inside. He was in a dark space with a desk, a chair, and little else. Rhythmic chanting sounded low from somewhere in the building. He crept to the door on the opposite wall and cracked it open.

The changes were coming from black-robed figures that filled the narrow room. An altar took center stage on the side wall. The room was lit by a multitude of candles. A pentagram was etched in the wall behind the altar.

When a woman began to speak, Billy felt his skin crawl. It was Dr. Clark.

"The sacrifice has arrived," she declared, as she walked through a doorway that connected the two businesses, the loud cries of the infant she carried announcing her arrival.

A sound from the back alley caused several of the cloaked figures to turn their attention toward Billy's hiding space. He moved swiftly to the shadows and tucked himself beside the wall and the desk. Several men moved through the room.

"Nobody's here." One man announced. "Must have been an animal."

Dixon? Billy knew his partner's voice but was still shocked to hear it.

Another voice in the darkness asked, "You sure you called off the cops tonight?"

"Yeah," Dixon sounded cocky. "I took care of it. No one is coming."

"What about your partner?"

Dixon scoffed, "Chief pulled him from the case."

"The Feds?"

"I took care of Malik. They won't find him for days. Wright is with us. Relax, man. I said I took care of it."

They walked back to the group, failing to secure the interior door.

Billy sat in stunned dismay. *That's why they're not here? Because of Dixon? Did he kill Malik?* He evaluated his options. Knowing his daughter was there meant there was no way he was leaving without her. He just had to find her.

Fifty-Two

Billy slipped back into the alley. He realized the two businesses were connected by the door that Dr. Clark had come through. He had to get into the building next door. That could be where they were holding Esther.

He moved quickly along the wall, standing in the shadows. In a few steps, he found the back entrance to the fish market. He tried the door. This time it was locked. He was about to break the glass when he heard a soft scuttling behind him.

Turning around, Billy caught a flash of yellow. Tucked behind the large blue dumpster, a small child whimpered. Billy moved quickly and, kneeling, reached for the child. His heart leaped, and tears sprang to his eyes as looked down to see his precious daughter, bound and gagged.

Freeing her from the zip ties and removing the gag, Billy wept. He found himself lost for words, only able to whisper her name. He drew her tightly to his chest.

"Daddy? Daddy! Oh, Daddy! I knew you would find me. I knew you would come! I prayed and prayed, and you found me!" She was laughing and crying and climbing onto his knee. "Daddy, Cassie. Can you save Cassie? She's in the smelly freezer." She plugged her nose for dramatic effect.

"Cassie?" he asked her. "Cassie is here?"

"Yes, in the smelly freezer," she repeated, this time pointing to the back door of the fish market.

Gunfire erupted in the building behind them. Billy muffled Esther's cry with his hand. "Shhh!" he whispered frantically. With eyes wide, she stopped screaming. Her breathing was erratic. He held her close. "I need you to hide, Esther. To be brave for a little longer. Can you do that?"

Her eyes were wide, but she nodded. "Yes, Daddy. I can be brave because you are brave." She traced her finger down the side of his face. Billy pulled her into a tight embrace. *Oh God, this kid! She is amazing. Thank You for keeping Your hand on her!* They moved down the alley, and Billy tucked her in a doorway cloaked in shadow, as far from the Wisdom Foundation as he dared to go. "Stay right here in this corner, baby girl. Don't move until I come back."

Billy dragged himself away from her presence, calling in to the station. "I'll go find Cassie. But you stay here. Don't make a sound now, and I will be back for you soon. Very soon, I promise." He was torn leaving her but needed to see if he could keep his promise to Cassie. Looking back several times, he ensured she stayed hidden.

Billy slowly approached the back door of the Wisdom Foundation. His gun drawn and ready, he slowly cracked open the door. He softly snaked through the opening and slid into the shadows. The interior door was still open thanks to Dixon and his friend. Billy inched closer to observe the space beyond.

He had heard the chaos that had erupted following the gunshots, and the members were still murmuring. But now the guards had the violator subdued. Billy recognized Ethan in the arms of the brutes.

"You can't do this, Draven. This is insane," Ethan protested until one more blow to the face silenced him.

"While he has killed one of our members, that makes a chance for one of you. Now's your chance, Detective." A man's voice cut through the madness. "As our newest member, you will take your place in our coven once you kill Ethan Walker." Standing at the altar, Draven Wolfe's face shone maniacally in the fiery glow of the candlelight.

Pulling his hood back and revealing his face, Dixon walked toward Ethan with a knife drawn. Without hesitation, he sank the blade into the man's side. Lifeblood spilled from Ethan as Dixon erupted with a terrifying shriek.

"Thank you, Ethan. By your life, I have secured my rightful place. I owe you a debt." Dixon leaned in and pulled the knife out of the wounded man's side.

Ethan spat in Dixon's face. "You won't get away with this," he whispered, a victorious smile on his face. Dixon left the man to a slow, painful death as he took his place in the circle.

"The sacrifice," Draven demanded.

Dr. Clark moved her large frame through the crowd. Billy moved in the shadows to see what she carried. He gasped when he saw the wailing infant, naked and cold, carried to the altar. He stared at Dr. Clark when she laid the baby on the stone. And all he could think of was his own infant son. A deep rage flooded Billy.

"And the girl's Bible!" she sounded triumphant as she smacked the black book onto the altar.

Billy remembered what Cassie had told him about the Bible. How she wrote down every detail she could remember. Obviously, Dr. Clark had not opened the book, or it would have been destroyed already.

In the distance, Billy heard the first faint sound of sirens. The cavalry was coming. But he had no time. He counted at least four heavily armed guards and another twenty to twenty-five people garbed in black. He had to think fast and act faster.

He slipped through the open door and crept closer to the circle, the shadows providing him ample cover. Draven began to chant as the others joined in. He spoke in an ancient language as he read from the dark book on the altar. They bowed their heads, and their dark hoods obscured their faces.

Numerous candles filled the room, and one was within reach of Billy.

Billy drew the candle toward him and lowered it to the robe of the closest member. Flames soon crept up the black shroud as the unwitting man began to dance and scream. His flailing arms hit another victim, whose cloak caught fire.

Havoc ensued.

Draven determined to continue the ceremony, chanting over the infant amid the pandemonium. Other members were shouting and scared.

From the shadows, Billy could see the fury on Harriet's face as she screamed at them all to calm down. Their collective turmoil covered the approaching sirens. Soon the flashing of lights signaled the end of the gathering.

As the men and women in blue descended upon the cult, Billy bolted for the infant on the altar, grabbing both the Bible and the child before Draven could complete the final sacrifice. Holding both, Billy checked on Ethan. A quick assessment determined the man could not be saved. He turned to run, but Ethan caught him by the wrist.

"Through there—" He pointed weakly to the door. "Cassie ..."

"I'll help her, Ethan," Billy said sternly. He had no desire to trust the man who was integral in making this all happen.

"I didn't know... I didn't." Ethan coughed as blood came pouring from his mouth.

Billy wasted no more time. Anticipating an alternate escape route, he raced through the door.

Harriet moved like a flash in the darkness. She was behind Draven with the sacrificial blade upon his neck. Driving the blade along his neck, she exclaimed, "I will ensure the sacrifice is made!" Two officers tackled her and wrestled the blade from her hand.

Billy bolted into the next room. Instead of an exit, he found the open door of the freezer and saw Cassie lying on the floor in a pool of her own blood. Holding the baby close to his chest, he shoved the Bible into his back pocket. He bolted to the front door of the market.

Yanking open the door, he cried, "I need assistance in here. Medics!"

Racing back to the freezer, he knelt beside the dying girl. "Cassie!"

In the other room, he heard his fellow officers making arrests, disarming the guards, and cuffing the participants of this disturbed group. He called out for medical assistance again. This time a female officer rushed through the door; another pushed a gurney through the main door of the Fish Market. They took over caring for Cassie and took the baby from Billy.

As Billy turned to go, a weak hand took hold of him. He leaned in to talk to Cassie, retrieving the Bible from his pocket.

"You are so brave, Cassie. You fought for all those kids. You protected my own little girl, Esther. And I have all the information you took down, right here." He tapped the Bible emphatically. "You fight for yourself now."

She tried to speak, and Billy bent closer to her.

"Nobody touched her."

Billy was confused for a moment.

"Esther." She began to drift. "God shielded her."

Even as the relief flooded him, Billy responded to the flash out of the corner of his eye. Someone had fled past him, headed for the back alley. He looked to his fellow officer.

"We've got this," the medic assured him. "Go!"

He didn't wait another moment. He burst out the back door into the alley and stopped short. A young girl was holding Esther by the back of her jacket.

"Daddy!" Esther cried out. "Missy, let me go!"

Missy wielded a long knife and drew it close to Esther's face. Esther stopped moving and softly whimpered as she went cross-eyed looking at the blade. Billy slowed his approach and kept his voice low and steady.

"Listen. If you let her go, I can help you. I can get you to safety, but you must let the little girl go," he crooned.

"No. Don't come any closer. I'll cut her; I swear I will." The black eyes that met Billy's sent a shock down his spine. *Not human!*

Esther reached her hand up slowly, and carefully released the zipper of her coat. She stomped hard on Missy's foot, causing her to react. Esther used the distraction and threw off the garment, leaving Missy holding an empty jacket. Rushing to her father, Esther pushed her legs as hard as she could until she reached his open arms.

The knife clattered on the ground as Missy dropped it and the coat and raced down the alley, lost in the shadows. Billy was more focused on his daughter than the runaway. He scooped her up in his arms and carried her back to the car.

Fifty-Three

Swerving in and out of traffic, Billy sped across town. He tapped Beth's icon on his phone, and the ringing began. He placed the call on speaker, and Beth answered on the second ring. "Billy! Is everything—"

"I've got her, Beth! I've got her!" Tears choked his words, and he cleared his throat. He handed the phone to Esther.

"Mama! Mama!" Esther began to cry.

Beth was weeping now, as well. "Baby, oh, Esther. I have been praying for you! I am so glad you are safe with Daddy."

"Mama, I was scared. But Jesus sent me an angel to protect me. She kept me safe the whole time."

Beth sighed into the phone, "He sure did, honey. Oh, I can't wait to see you."

Billy did his best to be sure she didn't have to wait long. Moments after Esther hung up the phone, Billy was pulling into the driveway. Both Beth and Maggie were waiting in the front yard to see their little loved one. Maggie was clinging to Beth's side.

As Esther pushed open the car door and climbed out, Maggie raced to her and nearly knocked her over. Beth tried to steady the girls, but they tumbled to the grass, crying, laughing, arms tight around each other. Billy joined the three of them on the grass. All together again.

"Oh, Esther. I'm so sorry I lost you," Maggie sobbed, speaking for the first time since her sister's disappearance.

"No, Maggie." Esther was firm for her tender years. "No, it wasn't your fault. She tricked you—that bad girl tricked you."

Beth knelt in front of her youngest. "Let Mama see you," she said, taking the girl by her shoulders. Billy, finally able to see her for the first time clearly, was shaken by the shape she was in. Her face was streaked with dirt and tears, her hair a tangled mess. He understood exactly why Beth's breathing had become ragged. He placed gentle hands on his wife's shoulders.

"She's home, Beth. God brought her home safe."

"Thank You, Jesus. Oh, thank You!" Beth spoke, her voice shaking.

Fifty-four

Cassie fidgeted nervously as she sat between Beth and Billy on the airplane. Heading back to Florida, to her parents, she just couldn't believe it. And she didn't know what to expect. It was her choice to fly home, rather than have her parents travel to her.

She longed to see them. She wanted to feel their arms around her. To be safe once again. She fought hard against the rising doubts that she was now tarnished and broken. Would they see her the same way?

Sitting by the window, Beth cooed and sang to the baby. Cassie hadn't named him yet. She barely could look at him, though she continued to pray for him. Her mind was in turmoil, and her heart was torn. How could she possibly raise this child who connected her to so much terror? She knew she could not.

She looked over at Billy, who smiled down at her. He was her rescuer, the one God had sent to find her. She still marveled at the stories Beth and Melody had regaled her with at the hospital. She saw clearly how God was speaking to them both in their dreams, and those moments were not just musings of her mind but visions from a loving God. It overwhelmed Cassie to think of how far God went to rescue her.

As the plane began its descent, the baby started to cry against the building pressure in his ears. Beth was ready with a bottle and had timed his schedule so he would be hungry enough to eat during the landing.

Upon arrival at the airport, they stood to exit the plane. Billy stepped out into the aisle to retrieve their luggage from overhead. He removed their suitcase as the girls pulled their backpacks and purses from under the seats. Cassie felt the panic begin to rise.

Billy stepped back to allow the ladies to exit the row, offering a hand to Beth as she climbed through the narrow aisle navigating the baby, her purse, and the large diaper bag.

"He is such a precious little thing." He smiled as she moved past him.

She nodded in response. "He sure is."

Cassie moved slowly down the narrow aisle in front of them. She heard the exchange and held it close to her heart. She paused at the door of the plane, taking a deep breath before exiting.

Beth came up behind her. "Are you all right, Cassie?" She adjusted her purse and the diaper bag to draw closer to Cassie. They walked down the ramp into the airport as fellow travelers swept past them.

Cassie took in a ragged breath. "I think so. I haven't seen them in a year. I … our last words …" Her voice trailed off as she held back the tears that burned her eyes. "We fought." She rolled her eyes in frustration against the growing doubts.

"It's okay, Cassie. It's okay. I know they love you. They are waiting for you. I'm sure they can hardly breathe thinking of this moment."

"How do you know?" Cassie asked.

"It's how I felt about Esther, and she was gone for just weeks. But when I held her that first time, there were no words, and I could just hold her and let the joy flood over me."

"But I'm …" Cassie hesitated to reveal her greatest fear. "I'm not the same. I'm broken. I'm used."

"But you are still *you*, Cassie," Beth reassured her. "You are still their little girl. And you have a road ahead of you in regard to healing. You don't have to be perfect; you don't have to be fixed. But they will help you find your way. They will help you with your healing."

Billy moved beside Cassie and gently took her hand. "Cassie, you are an amazing, smart, and resilient young woman. Parents who raised a girl like you will love you for eternity. Because of your quick thinking, we were able to identify all of Ethan's containers. We freed hundreds of children and brought closure to many more families. You protected Esther and consoled all those children in the midst of hell. *You* did that."

She smiled, confidence building as she headed down the narrow jetway into the airport. She began to breathe normally. *Lord, You were with me in the darkness. You are with me in the light. You have restored me and redeemed me. I know there is still a long journey of healing ahead of me, but I asked You to allow me to hug my parents again. Will they want to hug me?*

When they entered the airport, they followed the signs to the exit. Cassie had flown out of this airport with her parents many times since she was little. She led the way, barely reading the directional signs as she walked. She was picking up her pace, excitement building. She was finally allowing hope to bloom in her spirit.

As they passed through the final gates, Cassie saw that a large crowd had gathered. They erupted with cheers as Cassie made her way toward them. Poster board signs were designed with her name, "Welcome Home, Cassie." She scanned the multitude, all familiar faces. Friends, family, name and faces she knew and loved. But she looked for two faces … there! In the crowd, running toward her.

"Mom! Dad!" Cassie dropped her bag and raced into their open arms. "Oh, I'm so sorry." She sobbed, leaning into them. "I'm so sorry, Mommy. Daddy, I never should have—"

They both hushed her as they held her.

"No, oh, Cassie. Darling." Her mother's voice broke with emotion, as she stepped back to look her daughter in the face. "We are so glad you are home." She turned to her husband, and he continued for her.

"We prayed every night for you. We never gave up hope." He placed his arm around his wife and gave her a squeeze. "Your mom never stopped believing. Every day we watched and waited. And here you are. You are home." He took Cassie in his arms, "You are home." He stepped back and wiped his eyes.

Her mother clutched her to her chest, her arms strong and firm around her. Her father held them both, tears coursing down his cheeks. Finally, tears of joy.

After Cassie spent a few minutes greeting her friends and accepting promises to see them the next day, she headed home with her parents, the baby, Billy, and Beth.

They enjoyed Cassie's favorite dishes for dinner and talked late into the night. Beth shared the ways God had spoken to her and how she had prayed for Cassie without knowing her the whole time. Billy filled in many details of the case and how he found her. Cassie's parents wept—tears of sorrow to hear of all their daughter had endured mixed with tears of joy to have her back.

Their conversation was winding down. Cassie knew it was time.

"I am so thankful that God allowed my baby to live," she began. "I care for him." She paused. Even now, Beth was holding the child. "But I don't love him," Cassie continued. "He is a reminder of the horrible things that have happened. Now that I am home—" Cassie looked at her mom and knew the anger that they had shared was gone. "Now that I am home and back with my family, I want to move forward."

Beth held the child even closer to her. She dared not let her heart guess where Cassie was leading.

Cassie's lips quivered. She couldn't continue.

"It's okay, Cassie." Alexis hurt to see her daughter so distraught. "If you want to put him up for adoption …" She took her daughter's hand. "You can love him by sharing him with another family."

"You do still know me so well. I was so afraid …"

Her mom kept her close as she spoke. "No matter what you've been through, or will go through, you will forever be my girl, Cassie. Nothing changes that."

Cassie's breathing slowed. She squeezed her mom tightly and then turned to Beth and Billy. "I can't do it. I can't raise him. But it's not his fault." Cassie looked at Beth holding her son so lovingly and reached for him. She looked down at his face and smiled through fresh tears.

"Hello baby." Her voice was shaky. "I prayed for you. A lot. I protected you for as long as I could. I am sorry I can't be everything you need. But I know someone who can." With that, she looked up at Beth and gently passed the baby back into her arms. "Beth, Billy ... would you help me find a home for him?"

Beth's heart ached. A sob caught in her throat as her eyes burned. This child was not hers to bond with, and yet, he so reminded her of baby Will.

Billy looked at his wife. In her eyes was a desperate desire and a sense of hope and life that he hadn't seen for many months.

"Billy." She turned to him, hardly speaking above a whisper.

Billy wrapped his arm around his wife. "Of course we will, Cassie."

Cassie suddenly spoke out. "Beth, Billy, I know you lost your own baby ... If you ... would want to take this child, I know he would be loved. I know you would love him as your own."

Later that night, alone in the hotel, Beth curled in Billy's arm, her mind racing with so many thoughts.

"I know I can't have another child, but holding an infant again ... I know I will always grieve the loss of our baby, but one day, we will be reunited. I will hold him again, in heaven. But maybe here, on earth, we might consider—"

"I'd love that, Beth," he reassured her as he drew her closely to him.

"Billy," Beth burst out. "In all the dreams I've shared with you ... there is one thing I left out." Beth brushed the tears from her eyes. "Every time I saw Cassie, he was there. At first, I thought it was a message from God that my baby was safe with Him. That Will was cared for. But I realize now that it was *Cassie's* baby I dreamed of." She looked up at Billy. "We will raise him with great love."

"We will," Billy responded. He felt closer to Beth than he had in a long time.

Fifty-Five

Missy turned her collar to the wind as she sat hunched in the shadows of the alley. The summer storm brought cold rain, reflecting the feeling in her heart. Abandoned again. She was even angrier than before. She would never let another human being close to her. She would never allow another person to have any control over her.

She looked at the clock on the library annex across the street. Time to go. She stood up from her corner of the earth, grabbed the backpack she had stolen last week, and headed to the meeting spot. She just needed to make her way through the darkness until she was an adult. Renata still plagued her, but now Missy was in control. Refusing to commit to anything, she connected to no one, and she would split as soon as she wanted. Whether she needed to or not. It was going to be her way. Her decision. Her control.

Cassie watched as her mother washed the baby. She made it seem so effortless.

"Cassie." Alexis knelt beside the tub. "Can you get the new bottle of baby wash from the hall closet? I forgot to grab it before I got started. Unless you would rather hold—"

"Got it!" Cassie jumped up from the floor. She rummaged through the closet. Her mind had been so foggy. She wondered if she would ever be able to focus again. "What's the name of it? Oh wait, baby wash." She grabbed the bottle and handed it to her mother. She didn't care to look too long at the baby. His eyes were like hers, but so much was like James. She rubbed her hands over her arms, suddenly chilled.

Cassie watched as her mother cooed and tickled the baby and how he responded with a smile and a gurgle of his own. *I suppose I'm counting down the days to Beth's arrival more than she is.*

What she loved was all the time she had with her mom. The counselor was helping her work through the nightmares. Also the anxiety and depression. And the fear—and the desire to isolate. Cassie shook her head, attempting to cast out all the thoughts. Time with Mom. *Focus on one good thing at a time, Cassie. Mom is one very good thing.* Cassie allowed a smile.

Her mom looked up from the baby, "What are you smiling about, Cassie-girl?" she asked, using an old nickname.

"Just thinking about how you are my good thing."

Her mom set the baby in his bouncy seat and walked over to wrap her girl up in a big, mom-sized hug. "You are *my* good thing."

Cassie leaned into her mom. She felt so strong and so small at the same time. Her mom whispered truth and possibility as she held her. Cassie knew she would never be the same, but somehow ... somehow through God, there were still good things.

Has this story moved you? While the characters are fictitious, the portrayal of human trafficking is very real. Human trafficking is the fastest-growing criminal industry in the world. Millions of children experience human trafficking every year—and the majority are very young.

We can all do something to stand against this atrocity.

Please share this book! Send copies to every person who cares about our children! The first step to action is spreading awareness.

Then, visit Staceyherringbooks.com. You will find resources for parents, charities to support, and information to stay educated on human trafficking.

Remember the impact of a Bible study on Beth, Melody, and Mae? Starting a Bible study with friends is an excellent venue to hear God's direction. You will find my Bible study recommendations on this site too, such as *Women in the Bible Small Group Bible Study*, by Marina Hofman, PhD. Such studies strengthen our faith as we stand in the gap for God's children.

Visit Staceyherringbooks.com for all of these resources and more, and to connect directly with me!

Yours in the Fight for Children,

Stacey Herring

OTHER TITLES BY CASTLE QUAY BOOKS

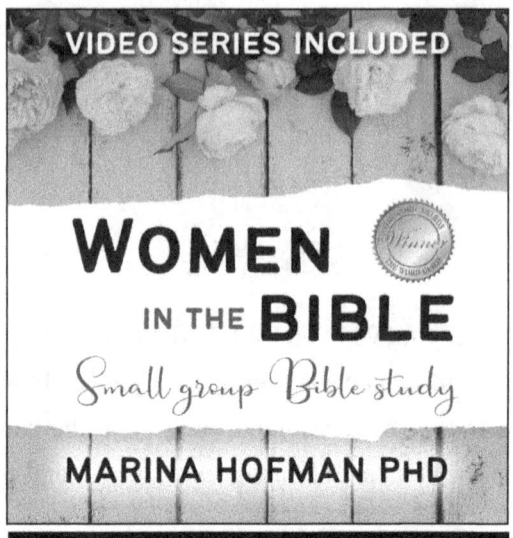

WOMEN IN THE BIBLE
Small group Bible study
MARINA HOFMAN PhD
VIDEO SERIES INCLUDED

THE TRUE STORY OF CANADIAN HUMAN TRAFFICKING
BY PAUL H. BOGE
FOREWORD BY PAUL BRANDT

AWARD WINNER
2019 Grace Irwin Award for Best Canadian Book of the Year
Debra Fieguth Award for Social Justice
Word Guild "General Market Award for Best Book –Life Stories" Category

CASTLE QUAY BOOKS